# Living in Paradox

*The Theory and Practice of
Contextual Existentialism*

## Ned Farley

**University Press of America,® Inc.**
**Lanham · Boulder · New York · Toronto · Plymouth, UK**

**Copyright © 2008 by**
**University Press of America,® Inc.**
4501 Forbes Boulevard
Suite 200
Lanham, Maryland 20706
UPA Acquisitions Department (301) 459-3366

Estover Road
Plymouth PL6 7PY
United Kingdom

Library of Congress Control Number: 2008930939
ISBN-13: 978-0-7618-4151-7(paperback : alk. paper)
ISBN-10: 0-7618-4151-2 (paperback : alk. paper)
eISBN-13: 978-0-7618-4265-1
eISBN-10: 0-7618-4265-9

# Table of Contents

List of Figures    v
Acknowledgements    vii
Introduction    ix

I:   Contextual Existentialism    1
     What Has Come Before    1
     An Existential Dilemma    4
     The Existential Paradoxes    5
     Out of the Shadows    6
     Contextual Existentialism Defined    17

II: The Nature of Paradox    19
     Ronnie    20
     Multiplicity    22
     The Existential Paradoxes    23
     Avoidance of the Moment    27

III: The Contextual Development of the Individual    29
     The Nature of Culture    30
     Relational Development    31
     Lonesome Sam    33
     Values Development    36
     Summary    38

IV:  The Use of Intuition    39
     The Intuitives and Homeostasis    40
     Gaby    42
     The Intuitives as a Mediator for Anxiety    44
     Summary    45

V:  Contextual Existential Assessment    47
     Foreground and Background    51
     Bryan    53
     Summary    58

VI:  Diagnosis, the DSM, and Language    59
     What is Diagnosis?    60
     A Process, Not an Outcome    61
     A Shared Language    62
     Back to Bryan    63

Conclusion                                               65

VII: Treating the Whole Person                           67
    The Case of Lonny                67
    Summary                          81

VIII: Working with Couples                               83
    The Case of Peter and Rachel     84
    Summary                          100

Afterward (and AfterWords)                               101
    The Clinician's Journal          101
    Illuminata                       102
    Final Thoughts                   106

References                                               109
Index                                                    111
About the Author                                         115

# List of Figures

Figure 1: Life In Balance                                     11

Figure 2: Life out of Balance                                 12

# Acknowledgements

As I have taught Existential Psychology over the years, I have come to find it hard to not allow my own interpretations to be present. Keep in mind here that I work on a campus that predominantly serves an adult population, many who are returning for their graduate degrees either to update their credentials or to change careers. This being said, understand that this learner population does not passively sit and soak up the pearls of my wisdom. They challenge, they speak from their own experiences, and they ask critically thought out questions. I am always careful to state my biases, even as I attempt to teach the basic philosophical and psychological concepts. Being the phenomenologist that I am, as students ask questions, I find myself needing to clarify and elucidate how I interpret and practice this belief system and approach to therapy. They are interested in where these ideas come from and how I have come to see certain concepts as important to my work. They often want very specific examples of how these ideas are put into practice. This "learning loop" of teaching and learning simultaneously, has evolved into this book.

I want to especially thank Seow Ling Chua for her meticulous attention to the details of editing and formatting in order to bring this book into reality; to Kathy Offner for her help in making my visual representations of theory actual graphics; and to Michael for his continuous support and belief in my ability to do this. Finally it is with profound thanks to my clients, my students and my teachers that I introduce Contextual Existentialism.

# Introduction

"Living never wore one out so much as the effort not to live."
--Anais Nin

As I begin to write about the emergence of the ideas that would shape the development of Contextual Existentialism, I am reminded of two specific experiences early in my career as a psychotherapist. The first was in 1985 and I had been working in community mental health providing crisis intervention and counseling to a fairly diverse population of mostly adults in an urban environment. My training to this point had been primarily Cognitive-Behaviorally focused, except for a brief introduction to Rogerian theory during my crisis intervention training. I was sitting with a young man in his early twenties. He was white and gay and terrified of coming out and "destroying" his relationship with his family. I kept trying to get him to "re-think" his assumptions about what might happen if he did, indeed, come out. I even tried to help him strategize some ways to approach the subject. I was working within a fairly cognitive frame. He just stared at me. As I look back at this now, I suspect he wondered what planet I came from, and questioned whether I had any concept of what his experience was in that moment. It didn't matter that I had a good understanding of the coming out process, or that I could call upon personal experiences of my own to connect with him. What mattered is that I wasn't *listening* to him, *his* story, *his* experience as it played out in that moment. If I had been, I might have been able to notice that what was really going on had less to do with coming out, and more to do with *who he was*, or more accurately, *who he was becoming*.

My second experience was shortly after this, perhaps within the next few months. I was sitting in supervision with my clinical supervisor, discussing cases. As I spoke about the work I was engaged in with my clients, I became acutely aware of how exhausted I was. Ordinarily, I wouldn't have brought this into the supervision, as it certainly didn't fit what I had been taught supervision was all about. However, on this day, during this time, it was such an acute feeling that it spoke for me. It was out of my mouth before my mind knew what was coming. Or so it seemed at the time. My supervisor paused for a moment, then, with a smile on his face said, "Of course you're tired. What do you expect when

you keep trying to fix your clients? Your attempts to make them feel better allows them to come in, dump their emotional baggage, and leave. They of course,
feel better . . . at least for a few days. You, on the other hand, feel tired. How
long do you suppose you can carry their work for them? Are you really helping
them?"

Well, needless to say, that set off an internal warring conversation for me.
Of course I was supposed to make them feel better, isn't that what therapists do?
Yet, on the other hand, his words struck a chord deep within me. They plowed
deeply into my own narcissistic belief that I actually had the power to make
anyone feel anything. In retrospect, a few years later while reading Irvin Yalom's *Existential Psychotherapy* (1980), I came across his discussion of ways in
which clients avoid making choices to live their lives authentically. He speaks
about clients who "dump and run." Although Yalom doesn't speak to the outcome of this for therapists, it was a pivotal moment for me as I came to understand what I have come to see as energetic transference, and the importance of
the body in the therapeutic process.

These two experiences, in hindsight, were critical moments in my understanding of my evolving beliefs about theory and therapy. It was these experiences, and many more over the early years of my career that ultimately led me to
my own growing awareness of existential anxiety and the ways in which it
manifests in our lives. More specifically, combined with my growing interest in
stretching western psychological theories to be more culturally useful, they
clarified my own theoretical bias about human beings, their growth and desire
for health and led me to understanding a more holistic approach to this work.

## Practice into Theory into Practice

I have been studying and teaching about Existential Psychology for the
past 15 years. Originally trained in Cognitive-Behavioral theory during my undergraduate and early graduate work, I found the tools useful as a clinician;
however, the theory itself left me cold. I had a sense that the human "being" was
left out of the equation; and that the focus on cognitive processes and behavior
dealt well with the symptoms, but rarely with the person experiencing those
symptoms. In my on-going journey of understanding the psychology of human
beings, I explored traditional and neo-Freudian psychoanalytic theory, other
branches of cognitive and behavioral theories, the somatic psychologies, and
humanistic and transpersonal theories. What I found is that some of these theories focused on our affect, that is, how we feel about the world around us and
ourselves. Others focused on spiritual crisis or on the physical/somatic aspects
of our being. All these spoke to different aspects of what it means to develop as
a person in this world, yet there always seemed to be important components left
out of the picture. Being someone who tries to think about the "whole person" I
explored systems theories, yet even here, the attention on the "system" often left
out the individual within the system. In fact, by the very nature of identifying

what the "system" was, these theories too, became dualistic in nature.

In the course of this time, I had also been exploring my own sense of spirituality and meaning. Having been raised as a Roman Catholic, I had years of experience in a religious tradition. However, I never felt comfortable with the dogma of formal religious teachings, especially when I experienced them as being counter to my own intuitive understanding of my spiritual self. I believe that one's spiritual nature is deeply personal, and should be defined and connected to in a personal way. For some that may mean through the structure of a formal religion or belief system, for others it may be through connecting to nature, or through one's own created sense of meaning making. Ultimately, I believe that spirituality and meaning making are synonymous. This not withstanding, I came to a belief that making meaning in one's life seems to be of paramount importance in the construction of a healthy personality.

My own journey led me to Zen Buddhist philosophy, as well as exploring both my Celtic and Native American heritages. What I found strikingly similar in these was a belief in the human being as constantly seeking balance, and like the existential concept of homeostasis, that our movement toward balance was deeply embedded in our nature. In addition, within these belief systems there is a deep understanding and reverence for the paradoxical nature of the world. Rather than seeing the world in terms of dualism, these systems of belief regarded the human journey as an experience wrought with profound possibility; with awareness that all aspects of our being encompass both the good and the bad, the masculine and the feminine, the right and the wrong. It is our willingness to accept this and to make our choices in life accordingly that affords us the gift of living a meaningful and balanced life.

It was during this personal exploration that I also was introduced to the psychology of Existentialism, both the European and North American versions. I felt as if I had come home! The ideas and concepts that were at the core of this theory spoke to the kinds of questions that I not only asked myself, but also heard in both overt and covert ways with my clients. This approach to being human not only seemed to capture my own experience of being in the world, but also seemed to hold a space large enough for the ideas and concepts held by other psychological theories. It was in this circle that I began to pull together the many facets of my understanding of being human and the nature of healing in a psychological framework. There was room here for all of whom I experienced myself to be, and how I found myself working with my clients.

Existentialists, both philosophers and psychologists or psychotherapists have come to honor sometimes seemingly divergent ways of understanding and explaining the core elements of this theoretical model. Although different writers and theorists have focused more heavily on one or another of the core concepts, we do all agree that certain ideas are central to any understanding and practice of existential psychology. Depending upon whom one is reading or studying, different aspects of existential thought may be in the forefront or the background. It is important for each of us to make sense of the puzzle, so to speak, and to find a way to make use of the concepts if we are drawn toward the ideas in general. Yet, in our haste to avoid creating yet another dogmatic approach, I wonder if we have cheated ourselves in standing firmly in what we believe in? Ultimately, of course, as I studied Existential Psychology in more depth, I came to see areas not addressed as overtly as I feel they should be. In my interpretation of Existentialism, I believe that the whole person *is* addressed; however, I believe that it is easy to overlook certain aspects that are crucial to working with others.

It is here that I want to present to you the fruits of my own process. From the core concepts of existential thought, to the ideas generated by other psychological theorists that I believe have a place in making sense of the human experience, to my own life experience and process, I have come to a way of thinking about and practicing the art of existential therapy. Finally, the profound impact of my spiritual and meaning-making life also contributes to ways in which I view my understanding and practice of counseling and psychotherapy. It is in acknowledging these influences, and the refinements of my own understanding of existential theory, that I have come to this place of offering a model for understanding and working with others and ourselves.

In Chapter 1, I will introduce an overview of the traditions of existential psychology, including a brief description of its roots in philosophy. I will then move on to explain the core concepts of Contextual Existential theory. Chapter 2 will discuss the role of paradox and how in particular, Zen Buddhist concepts such as mindfulness and Native American views of holism can be utilized within this theory. Chapter 3 will outline my understanding of the contextual development of the individual, specifically addressing both relational and values development. Chapter 4 will introduce my understanding of the role of intuition as a critical component of theoretical and practical understanding. Chapters 5 and 6 will discuss how Contextual Existential theory utilizes both assessment and the language of diagnosis both as practical tools, and as a language for communicating with others practicing from divergent theoretical models. Chapter 7 will specifically address therapy with individuals, and Chapter 8 with couples, and by extension, families. Finally, the Afterward will bring the reader full circle and encourage thinking about and utilizing a Contextual Existential frame beyond the therapy room.

# I

# Contextual Existentialism

"There is no justification for present existence other than its expansion into an indefinitely open future." Simone de Beauvoir

## What Has Come Before

One of the unique features of Existential Psychology is its roots in the philosophy that arose simultaneously (one might even say synchronistically) in the thoughts and ideas of many different individuals at roughly the same time, in all parts of Europe (Barrett, 1958). As one looks at the historical and social nature of the time (the latter 1800's and early 1900's), the Western world was experiencing a radical shift away from an agrarian society and toward an industrial one. People were figuratively being torn from their roots, their connection to the earth and their communities, and being driven toward urban areas and work in factories, refineries and other more detached arenas of labor. This sense of disconnection disrupted one's life, and in turn created an opportunity for human crisis to emerge. Although most certainly always evident in human existence, this new crisis, felt particularly strongly in Europe, opened up an intense level of anxiety, both within the individual and within the culture at large. With the experience of not one, but two World Wars fought on their soil, it forced open at a higher level the need to re-examine not only one's relationship to others and the world, but one's meaning and value in the world. In addition one's sense of making choices and the inherent responsibilities that this engenders, as well as one's sense of identity in the world as one grapples with the recognition of our mortality even as we strive to live our lives fully, also begged for exploration. This profound understanding of the relationship between our inner and outer worlds; of the recognition that not only our biological world, but other aspects of our environment (politics, cultural factors, social norms, family, religion, etc.) played an enormous role in how we constructed our lives; opened the door to a new way of understanding ourselves as human beings.

In its original forms, existentialism arose as a philosophical approach to understanding the human condition, yet quickly it became apparent to several individuals that it had profound psychological significance. Specific thinkers contributed enormously to the ideas that evolved into what we know now to be Existential Psychology. While a history of existential thought almost always includes such writers as Martin Buber, Albert Camus, Miguel de Unamuno, Jose Ortega y Gasset, and Nikolai Berdyaev; the works of Soren Kierkegaard (and it should be recognized that much of Kierkegaard's work became known in large part because of Karl Jaspers), Martin Heidegger, Frederich Nietzche, and Jean-Paul Sartre are considered the strongest influences in the development of Existential Psychology (Barrett, 1958; Yalom, 1980).

Kierkegaard, a Danish philosopher, contributed to our understanding of existential concepts such as the "I Am" experience, choice (freedom) and responsibility, "truth as subjective," and in his major work *Fear and Trembling* (1986), the struggle with "Being and Nothingness," a treatise on the eternal struggle with our death awareness. Heidegger, a German philosopher, offered us insight into concepts such as Husserl's phenomenology, "man's alienation from self," and the dualistic nature of subjectivity and objectivity (and our need to move beneath it). In addition, he wrote extensively on the meaning of existence, our experience of death anxiety, and temporal reality. *Being and Time* (1962) is perhaps one of his most noted contributions. Nietzsche, a German academic who taught Greek philosophy early in his career, offers us his discussion of power and nihilism (one's capacity for self-destruction) and conversely, one's "will to power" (being and becoming), most notably in *Thus Spake Zarathustra* (1978). Finally, Sartre, a French novelist and playwright, explored the human capacity for self-transcendence (becoming fully who we can be). His most passionate work of non fiction is *Being and Nothingness* (1993), which speaks most clearly to his focus on the underlying anxiety that propels us towards our potential. Yet it is in his fiction, his plays *No Exit* (1947/1976) and short stories, such as *The Wall* (1945/1975), that his struggle for self-creation and self-transcendence is most pronounced.

Others, such as Melard Boss and Ludwig Binswanger, contributed more specific ways in which these existential concepts translated into analytic practice (Barrett, 1958). In addition, there is recognition of how these ideas were represented in the creative processes as well; an understanding that the anxiety generated by this shift in experience could not always be articulated in academic or philosophical writings. Thus, expression through the poetry and prose of writers such as Anais Nin and Simone de Beauvoir, of novelists like Doestoevsky and Camus, the plays of Sartre, and the emergence of the art movements of Cubism, Dadaism and Surrealism, all came to be understood as existential expressions of personal and cultural angst.

Lest it be said that Existentialism is solely a European phenomenon based on the European experience, it is important to remember that industrialization became a worldwide phenomenon. Certainly in North America, particularly in the United States and Canada, this experience was also occurring. The effect here was predominantly post World War II, with the influx of another generation of immigrants, mostly from war-torn Europe, who along with their hardiness came their deeply felt experiences. Add this to the post war North American experience, and you have what could be called North American Existentialism. Tempered by the "can do" philosophy and culture of the United States and Canada, North American Existential thought was more optimistic, yet still grounded in the reflective understanding of the root causes of human anxiety and distress. After all, it was oppression and suffering that brought most of our ancestors to these shores, many seeking freedoms and a new way of life; others brought here by force. It should be noted that for many who study Existential philosophy and psychology, the inclusion of the American, William James, is seen as integral. Although commonly placed in the Pragmatic School, James in many ways really fits better into the existential frame. His writings, which had a major influence on later psychological development (he pre-dates Freud on many topics), expounded freely on such existential concepts as paradox, temporal reality, subjectivity, and the transcendant experience (Frager & Fadiman, 2005).

This inter-generationally understood knowledge, coupled with a belief that we can create our destiny, offered fertile ground for this new philosophical psychology. Writers and practitioners like Victor Frankl (1959/1984), Irvin Yalom (1980), Rollo May (1983), James Bugental (1987) and Clark Moustakas (1996, 1997) offered this more holistically oriented view of human nature to counter the strong hold that traditional and neo-Freudian analysis had in the psychological community. Rather than a more deterministic perspective on human experience, the existentialists offered the concept that humans are whole to begin with, and naturally seek balance (or homeostasis). With an understanding that our body, mind, emotions, and (depending on the writer) our spiritual natures are all connected, the focus became one that looked at the givens of our existence, rather than our animal instincts as the force that drives the conflicts within ourselves. Rather than explaining some inner struggle between our conscious and unconscious in response to our instinctual need to survive and pro-create, the existentialists looked at how the individual must come to understand his/her role in the eternal struggle between creating our own life and the underlying tension that we all experience as a given of being human in our world. Most notably, these "givens of existence" are our struggles with isolation and the desire to be connected, the striving toward finding meaning in a world that often feels meaningless or in contradiction to our beliefs and values, to our understanding that with choice comes responsibility (an existential definition of true freedom), and our constant awareness (even when repressed) of our mortality as we strive to live our lives (Yalom, 1980).

In addition, existential psychologists (both European and North American), many of who had been trained and were grounded in the psychodynamic roots of analytic thought; came to see human beings as whole and healthy, not mere pawns in the struggle between our deterministic biology and our pathological responses to early childhood experience. Rather, with an understanding that early experiences certainly contribute to how we perceive and interact in our world, we are constantly striving to transcend our experiences and move toward a state of balance (physically, mentally, emotionally, and spiritually). With an inherent capacity for self-awareness, we strive for this homeostasis by responding to our anxiety; that state of being-ness that is a healthy response to our struggles between living in the world and the above mentioned givens of existence.

## An Existential Dilemma

Sawako is a 24-year-old Japanese-American who immigrated to the U.S. with her family when she was 4 years old. As such, she has grown up very much in American culture, yet at home, is strongly influenced by her parent's Japanese heritage. At this point in her life, Sawako is struggling to decide whether or not she wants to attend graduate school to become a nurse as her parents wish her to, or to continue to do the work she currently does as an interpreter in a social service agency which she loves. She comes to therapy to explore this dilemma after experiencing a severe depression that lasted for several months. She was offered anti-depressants from her doctor, but was not willing to try them at that point. Eventually she did, and found that they helped take the edge off of her symptoms, but did not seem to help her beyond that. Sawako has never been involved in therapy before, although she has acted as an interpreter for clients at her agency who are seeking therapeutic help.

As Sawako begins her work, her therapist, who is first generation Korean American, asks her to tell her story in her own way, specifically the story of her current experience of her life. As Sawako tells of her discomfort, her therapist encourages her to pay attention to her here-and-now feelings, body sensations, thoughts, images, and any other aspects of her experience that she is aware of. With gentle but direct guidance, Sawako begins to become aware of the tension she feels between what she values and believes about her life, versus her parents' values and expectations. She also becomes more aware of how she perceives that she has no choices in how her life will unfold.

Attending to, and noting Sawako's cultural history and experience, her therapist begins to explore how Sawako indeed has choices, and is making them every day in her life. Sometimes, these are choices that are quite evident, and other times as subtle as her choices about her attitude about something in her life. She even begins to see how choosing not to choose might be a choice. Being respectful of Sawako's cultural experience and understanding, her therapist asks Sawako to consider all of the possibilities and their potential consequences as she helps her to see that she has more power in her life than she was aware of. Ultimately, the work helps Sawako to weigh her options as she comes to feel more congruent and present in her life. She sees how anxious she gets around making choices, and also around making meaning in her life. This is natural. Her anxiety is actually a beacon by which she can transcend her experience with more awareness. It is, in fact, an energetic "fuel" if you will, that when harnessed, can help us create our future. She comes to understand that her depression in large part was a result of "choosing not to choose" and struggling with her evolving awareness of her own values and beliefs which did not always match what her parents wanted for her. As she begins to own this awareness, recognizing that choosing her life was still difficult, she experienced less depression and a greater sense of aliveness.

## The Existential Paradoxes

This case study points out one example of how this struggle is understood as paradoxical in nature. That is to say, our anxiety arises out of an understanding that these givens of existence are not dualistic in nature, rather tensions that must be held and transcended in order to create our future. We are both alone *and* striving for connection; we have the freedom to choose our lives *and* we are responsible for the consequences of those choices; we live in a world that often feels void of meaning *and* we are constantly searching for (and creating) what is meaningful and of value for ourselves; and finally we have constant awareness of our mortality (even if out of conscious awareness) *and* we attempt to live our life fully. While this case did not particularly speak to these last two paradoxes, chances are if we were to continue to explore Sawako's life over time, they would emerge.

When at some level, we become aware of one or more of these paradoxes, we most often creatively avoid the anxiety that emerges through a variety of defensive mechanisms. Within this avoidance, is also a choice to not live our lives in the present moment, but rather to focus on what has been, or what might be. This *past* or *future tripping* allows us to spend an enormous amount of energy avoiding our here-and-now experience, thus allowing life to live through us instead of dynamically living our life. This also moves us from our capacity for authentic living, that whole, healthy being who has the answers to any given circumstance; and instead we become slaves to our own neurosis, responding to our historical experiences and perceptions and/or projecting into our future all of the dysfunctional ways we have dealt with our anxiety.

With an inherent belief in the power of our will, and our ability to proactively meet our destiny head on, and thus create our future; existential psychology is the bridge between psychodynamic theory, which offers profound understanding of the power of our historical experience; and humanistic and transpersonal theories, which understands the subjective nature of these experiences and the capacity we have to change and grow; to re-find our core healthy potential. By taking the best of both schools of thought, existential psychology attempts to dive underneath the western tendency toward dualistic splitting; subject/object, good/bad, healthy/sick, right/wrong, conscious/unconscious; and offers a container that holds the paradoxes of our lived experiences and helps us to understand that living an authentic and congruent life is not only possible, but an innate capacity that we all have within us.

# Out of the Shadows

Even as I read what I have written to this point, I realize that of course, my rendering of the basic tenets of existential theory is, in itself biased. I, as have all of us, have interpreted the work of those who have written about this topic before me and made these ideas and concepts my own. Although I feel fully comfortable in my take on these concepts, and have no doubt that my peers in reading this will agree, at least in spirit, that I have captured the major points that existential theory tries to convey; I am also certain that I have not articulated the exact meaning that other writers might have intended. Fortunately, by finding myself playing in this theoretical field, I can also feel comfortable in knowing that subjectivity is honored and that for the same reason that I previously posed the question about the non-dogmatic nature of this theory, I can use this to my own advantage in defending my perspectives and interpretations. Thus, the paradoxical nature of the world emerges once again.

This being said, I would like to continue the discussion of the emergence of Contextual Existentialism by briefly sharing my thoughts about the areas that I have felt were/are not adequately addressed in the literature to date. My intent here is to provide an overview of these concepts, then to explore them more fully in later chapters. These are not presented in any specific order of importance.

## Early Childhood Development

Although existential theory itself was certainly influenced by Freud's work in psychoanalysis, it broke ranks on several fronts, not the least of which was the disagreement on what dynamic tension was at play as the root cause of anxiety. While Freud postulated the role of biology and determinism through the lens of our instincts (particularly Eros and Thanatos, our sexual and aggressive/survival instincts) (Freud, 1962); existential theory posited the role of being human and the tension that arises from dealing with the conditions of living in the world. In addition, existentialism focuses on the here-and-now experience of our lives, recognizing that whatever historical issues/behaviors are still unresolved will be played out in the present until they are resolved. This too, is a sharp departure from the concept that one must focus on past history in order to adapt to our present day experience. Coming from a pro-active health oriented perspective allows clinicians and clients to see the process as one of growth and change (*Becoming*) rather than mere adaptation to set patterns of behavior.

Nonetheless, psychoanalytic theory did offer us an understanding that our early childhood development was/is crucial to our current mode of living in the world. While Freud, and to some extent some of his theoretical descendants, focused primarily on sexual and social development, others, such as Klein (1957) and Winnicott (1971), moved in the direction of relational development. While not discounting the role that sexual and social development may play, from an existential perspective, the role of relational development seems crucial to consider, particularly as it relates to the core paradox of isolation and connection (although it certainly has impact on the other paradoxes as well). Earlier existential writers, while not negating the role of early childhood development, did not really overtly address this in the development of existential theory.

From a Contextual Existential framework, I would argue that understanding the role and nature of how we learn to relate to others and the world is crucial in both our assessment and treatment of the individual. Recognizing that we learn to relate primarily during our early years, and particularly are influenced by our interactions with our primary caregivers, I am drawn to the work of Karen Horney (1945), who along with the Object Relations theorists, studied caregiver-child interactions, and looked at the patterns that emerged in terms of relational styles. I am drawn to Horney's perspective because she moved away from seeing this early learning as only the product of mother-child roles (broadening it to see the role of any significant caregivers), as well as shifting to an understanding that these early patterns, while significant, are not unchangeable. In addition, her attention to the role that gender and culture play in one's development is conducive to a contextual approach. The fact that she was influenced by the writings of William James and Soren Kierkegaard, both existentialists, is certainly not to be overlooked as well.

In short, her coining of the terms *compulsive compliant, compulsive detached*, and *compulsive aggressive* (Horney, 1945) are useful and important in our understanding of the way in which we all have come to learn how to relate. In our striving for connection, we must move within a world that is often unsafe, if not outright hostile. Within a healthy and loving environment we learn how to relate to others and the world based on what will keep us in a state of balance. When threatened, the ability to detach, be aggressive, or be compliant may all be appropriate responses depending on the specific situation. Our ability to move with fluidity between these responses is essential to maintaining healthy balance. When we are raised in an environment where care giving is conditional at best, we learn to depend more heavily on one of these styles of relating more than the others, in direct response to the unhealthy behaviors of our primary caregivers. This more rigid use of relational styles, while working to keep us safe as children, ultimately begins to get in the way as we grow up. This results in dis-ease in our ability to relate to others and the world, and creates neurotic tendencies towards isolation, enmeshment, or aggression; none of which allows us to find healthy relationship. By assessing the client's primary styles of relating, we have a clearer picture of how they deal with the isolation/desire for connection paradox, thus increasing our ability to work with them successfully at dealing with the existential anxiety that arises naturally within this paradox. When we have an unhealthy relational style, we are out of balance. When we are out of balance in this way, we have difficulty dealing with the healthy anxiety that arises in relating, thus increasing our chances of attempting to avoid this anxiety, which then becomes neurotic.

## Values Development

The paradox of meaning and meaninglessness is another important tenet of existential theory. While many writers have discussed the role of meaning making within the existential framework, most notably Victor Frankl and his work in Logotherapy (1959); a discussion of the development of values or ethics is only cursorily addressed. There is much discussion of the role of values and ethics as a component of living an authentic life however the focus is on the *role,* not the developmental process itself. Soren Kierkegaard, in *Fear and Trembling* (1954, 1986), talks specifically about the levels of existence; all of which have clear parallels to other developmental models, and can be used quite effectively to discuss a model of values development. His discussion of the aesthetic level, the ethical level, and the religious level are helpful in understanding how we come to learn about moral/value/ethical issues, as well as how we respond to conflicts that arise from these issues.

From a Contextual Existential perspective, I would again argue that including a model of development that specifically addresses the formation of values and ethics is highly important in understanding how we come to construct meaning in our lives. By understanding how individuals move through and/or become stuck in these developmental levels, we are better prepared to help them identify problems and neurotic tendencies within the meaning/meaninglessness paradox, thus more likely to help them regain balance and deal with the healthy anxiety that is expected within this paradox.

## Spirituality

For a significant number of people who have studied psychological theory, existential psychology has often been interpreted as a philosophy and approach rooted in an anti-religious or anti-spiritual dialogue. Quite to the contrary, when studied more thoroughly, it is recognized as a theoretical approach that is often deeply spiritually connected. The paradox of meaning/meaninglessness is not only ripe, but the logical arena in which to explore spiritual values. One needs only to read some of the early existential writers to see a strong spiritual influence. For example, both Buber (1970, 1996) and Kierkegaard (1986) were strongly religious in their writing about the spiritual crisis inherent in being torn from our grounded ness. Even Nietzsche, in his "God is dead" statement, although a self-proclaimed atheist, yearns for a god figure (whether Dionysian or not) (in Barrett, 1958). Here, he is mirroring the overwhelming sense by many during the tumultuous times in Europe after industrialization and in response to war, that humankind had been separated from God, that one's beliefs in God as savior had been shaken. It brought to the forefront the question of what is our role in creating our lives. It spoke to the responsibility that we each have to make choices in our lives that allow our destiny to unfold, to live our lives authentically.

Granted, early existential psychologists did not speak very clearly to the role of spirituality in existential theory; perhaps because in their own experiences it was so clearly seen. Nonetheless, in the growing body of literature, meaning making was not clearly connected to spiritual belief systems. Generally speaking, the notion of meaning making and the paradox of meaning/meaninglessness was left open to interpretation, such that one could see it from a secular humanistic perspective, or on the other end of the continuum, from a more traditional religious perspective. One's interpretation was subjective and individual in keeping with the principles of the theory. Thus with the language of the *Umwelt, Mitwelt,* and *Eigenwelt,* clarifying the roles of the biological world, the inner world of the individual, and the relational world; there is an assumption that the spiritual world is covered. It was not until Van Deurzen-Smith added the term *Überwelt* (1988) that we had a more clearly articulated and overt understanding of the important role that spirituality plays in this theory.

From a contextual existential perspective, the addition of the Überwelt is crucial. From this, we interpret spirituality and one's spiritual nature to mean anything involved in one's perception of how one makes meaning in life. Thus, one can be an atheist or agnostic and see meaning making from a purely secular perspective. One also can bring in any spiritual or religious tradition to this, seeing deep connections between one's relationship to a higher power, higher state of consciousness, or connection to the earth as the motivating force in how one makes meaning of their life and existence. However, Contextual Existentialism goes farther, in its discussion of how one experiences and integrates making meaning into one's life. By including Zen Buddhist and Native American concepts, particularly in reference to their approach and understanding of the spiritual nature of humankind's deep connection to each other, the planet, and the universe that holds us all, clinicians and clients can have some practical ways in which to address spirituality in their lives. By utilizing the Zen principles of mindfulness and the practice of meditation, along with the Native American principles of holism and inter-connectedness within the circle of life as therapeutic concepts, there is an easy connection to the role of spirituality in our pursuit of homeostasis.

## Homeostasis as Balance between the Body, Mind, Emotions, and Spirit

Existential psychology sees the core motivation of human existence as the natural drive toward homeostasis or balance. However, in the literature to date, clarification of what this balance means is not easily evident. It is interpreted in the broadest sense as a frame that understands that human beings are born in a state of health, which we consistently try to maintain even under adverse circumstances. This healthy state of being-ness certainly involves our biology as well as our psychology, and is often derailed due to external environmental influences, such as from unhealthy family or social interactions. Other levels of understanding homeostasis include one's ability to recognize and utilize healthy anxiety, which arises when confronted with the previously mentioned givens of existence. When we succumb to this anxiety and, through either denying or avoiding it, allow it to become neurotic, we move out of balance and respond to our world and life in unhealthy ways.

Contextual Existentialism posits that we utilize this basic understanding of homeostasis and take it one step further. We need to come to understand that balance is ultimately experienced when we address the four domains of being-ness clearly and overtly: the mind (that which deals with cognition's and perceptions; our thought processes); the body/soma (both an understanding of our innate biology as well as the role of our physical self in how we relate to the world); the emotions (how we respond to the world at a feelings level); and the spirit (that understanding of ourselves and our place in the universe that guides us in making meaning, thus in our actions) (see Figure 1).

We are out of balance when we over utilize one or more of these domains at the expense of the others. This can be seen clearly when assessing which paradoxes are in the foreground for an individual, and what mechanisms are being utilized to avoid dealing with the anxiety. Neurotic behavior and responses to the world can be seen as a direct connection to this out-of-balance use (or lack of use) of these domains (see Figure 2).

Furthermore, it should be noted that although we use the terms "balance" and "homeostasis" interchangeably, there are subtle differences that are important to understand. The concept of balance often elicits an image of equal parts. Homeostasis understands that in the largest picture (and over time), we are attempting to equalize the various aspects of our state of being. However, it is perfectly within reason (and in the natural world, a "norm") that at any given moment, homeostasis might look like being out-of-balance. It is only when we understand the subtle changes occurring from moment to moment that we can see that it is the process, not the end result that reflects a truly "balanced" being. Yet from this moment to the next, to the next, it is natural and necessary to compensate within our domains of mind, body, emotions, and spirit to respond to our world. Paradox is seen again, we are both out-of-balance and striving for homeostasis at all times. We are perfectly imperfect.

Figure 1

# LIFE IN BALANCE

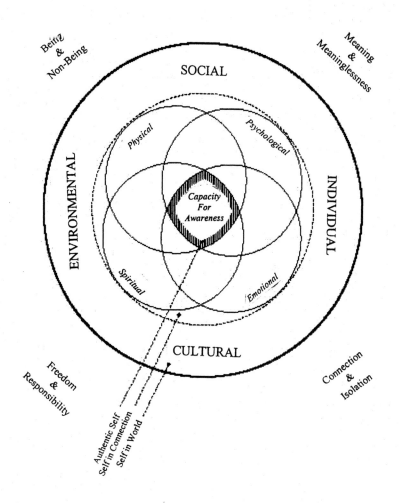

Figure 2

# LIFE OUT OF BALANCE

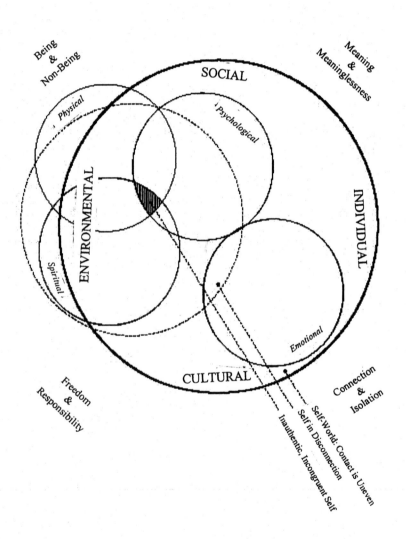

## Foreground/Background

The concepts of foreground and background are not new. Other theories have utilized these concepts to discuss how one understands the connections between specific behaviors and their psychological causes. What is the underlying reason that behavior *x* is occurring? Contextual Existentialism utilizes this concept to both understand causality and connection, but adds to it the usefulness of the concept in assessing what within the therapeutic relationship is the client's and what is the clinician's. Understanding that healing happens within the therapeutic relationship and that this inter-subjective experience is essential to the healing process; identifying what we each bring to this process in order to "create" this new relationship is crucial.

The "background" in this case is that which speaks to the client's experience, inclusive (as examples) of which of the domains is being over utilized in the moment, such that we can have a starting place to work towards integration and balance. Also important is understanding which and how one of the paradoxes might be most at work in a client's presenting problems. At yet another level, this allows us to help guide the client toward homeostasis in their life. The "foreground" here speaks to the therapist's experience being with the client, being aware of and attending to his/her own here-and-now process as it unfolds within the inter-subjective frame of therapy. In many ways, the psychoanalytic language of transference can be useful here, although, as will be discussed later on in this book, how we define and understand the transferential process will be different.

## Assessment and Diagnosis

Historically, existential clinicians have been averse to utilizing formal assessment as a tool to help guide their clinical work. At the heart of this argument is the understanding that one works in the present moment. Thus assessment is not practical, in that it (usually) has been a tool that primarily explores history. In the same vein, diagnosis has been seen as pathologizing the client as well as labeling a client's problems in such a way as to freeze him/her in time and not allow for an understanding of the here-and-now focus of the work, as well as the continuously evolving nature of growth and change. Yalom, in his book *Existential Psychotherapy* (1980) is one of the few clinicians that argue for the inclusion of a more formal clinical assessment role in therapy.

These are appropriate critiques of the traditional analytic and cognitive-behavioral models of psychology; which tend more often than not to buy into the medical model definition of pathology. Yet, I wonder if in our zeal as humanists to deny the role of assessment and diagnosis as tools of the evil empire, we perhaps have missed an opportunity to re-define both the role of assessment and diagnosis, of how one can utilize this information. Contextual Existentialism chooses to see value in both assessment and diagnosis, yet to utilize these tools as background for the work itself. They can provide us, through an existential lens, some ways of understanding our clients experience and what has formed these experiences. This is clearly in line with a phenomenological approach. The difference is that then we must put them off to the side and listen for the client to tell us what is going on for them. These tools are for *our* use, to frame a beginning understanding of what is out of balance in a given situation, yet we must always be open to let our interpretation go as each moment unfolds, and our clients tell their stories. Contextual Existential assessment addresses the importance of how we understand our client's stories through a theoretical lens; thus what we assess is specific to this theoretical bias.

As for diagnosis, I see sharing a common language as useful when discussing cases with my colleagues. My interpretation of diagnostic categories will always come from my contextual existential lens. My understanding of how and why these symptoms manifest will differ from many of my colleagues, yet we can understand each other when we use the language of diagnosis to explore specific symptoms. Seeing the Diagnostic and Statistical Manual (DSM) (APA, 2000) as a foreign language helps us to avoid labeling our clients, and recognizing that it is human beings who "label," not the language of diagnosis itself.

## Mindfulness and the Nature of Mind

Existential theory has superbly addressed the role of being in the here and now as fundamental to both understanding and working within this framework. Attending to the relationship between therapist and client, and keeping the work in the present has been clearly articulated. What has not been adequately addressed in my mind is how we come to understand what the here-and-now experience is. Here again, the influences from Zen Buddhist and Native American practices can contribute to our work. Within Zen Buddhist philosophy and practice lays a deep appreciation for the concept of mindfulness, that ability to fully attend to the moment with focus and intentionality. Through predominantly meditative practices, one can learn to be mindful, to listen with the whole self to the here-and-now experience. It involves the mind, the body, the emotions, and the spirit working in unison to guide us towards understanding our experience. This easily parallels the Native American practices that focus on one becoming fully aware of his/her contextual experience and knowledge. Through practices such as sweat lodge, vision quest, and the use of medicine wheel and healing circles; individuals and communities become aware of whom they are and the role they play not only in their individual lives, but within the larger contextual world of family, community, and environment.

With a clear intention not to co-opt these cultural practices, the focus is on utilizing the profound knowledge these concepts offer within a Contextual Existentialism frame. By creatively responding to each individual client experience, the use of self-reflective and holistic/systemic interventions allows the clinician and the client to pay more attention not only to the "why" of an experience, but to the "how" of our process of understanding. Through cultivation of mindfulness, and attention to the inter-connectedness of all things in both the therapist and the client, we can enter into therapeutic relationship more fully, and experience the healing nature of relationship more fully, and I would suggest, more expediently.

## Use of the Intuitives

Another area that Contextual Existentialism addresses is the role of intuition, both for the therapist and for the client. Moustakas (1990) has discussed intuition as the bridge between our tacit knowledge (knowing/knowledge without words), and our ability to articulate consciously what we know and understand (our verbal language and behaviors). In my experience, I have also come to understand intuition as strongly connected to our senses. Rather than seeing intuition (like psychic ability) as the sixth sense (although on some level this might be an accurate definition); I see how intuition comes through our five senses: visual, auditory, kinesthetic, olfactory, and gustatory. I also have come to believe through my clinical experience, that most of us have a more highly developed "intuition" in one of these senses. I know mine is predominantly kinesthetically driven, although my visual is also highly active. I suggest that the therapeutic work is highly dependent on how well we recognize and can utilize our primary Intuitives in our work, as well as how we can help our clients recognize and utilize their own as part of their daily life. Specifically, how we can use these "senses" to guide us in our attempt to stay present in our work, and to listen to the underlying, often easily overlooked information that can be present and useful. Finally, I would argue that these Intuitives are, in fact, also the primary way in which we identify and understand the transference process in the therapeutic relationship. Later, in the chapter discussing the use of intuition in therapy, I will speak more to the way in which contextual existentialism speaks to transference as an energetic process.

## Paradoxical Thinking as a Tool

Contextual Existential theory strongly encourages the use of paradoxical thinking as a therapeutic tool. Although existential psychology has long understood the nature of paradox, little has been discussed outside of the use of paradoxical intention (basically, prescribing the opposite) as a tool of therapy. Again, both Zen Buddhist and Native American philosophies and practice offer us a more clearly articulated understanding of the nature of paradox, perhaps because it has been embedded in Eastern and most indigenous cultures worldwide more naturally and overtly. Either way, by helping both ourselves as therapists and our clients learn to think from a both/and perspective instead of in either/or ways, we can begin the healing process. When we come to think and live in the both/and perspective, we open our lives to countless possibilities. Thinking in this way leaves room for choices to present themselves. The either/or, dualistic way of thinking is limiting, both in thought and in action. Cultivating paradoxical thinking allows the healing process to move, especially during times of stress. There is less of a tendency to stay stuck, when we realize that there are inherently no "right" or "wrong" answers, only the answers that we know will lead us toward authentic and congruent living in our world. In addition, if we can aid ourselves, and thus our clients, to experience paradox as a holistic process (i.e. we can learn to identify the experience not only intellectually, but also emotionally, somatically, and spiritually), it offers an amazing array of choices for us to work with in our lives.

## The Concept of "Self"

Within existential theory, as well as most all of western psychological theory, there is the standard use of the concept of "self." In most cases, "self" is interpreted and used to describe the unique nature of one's individual being. Additionally, it is constructed as a static element, a core construct that is, by its very nature, set and unchangeable. Rather, western psychology seems constantly to be engaged in the process of "finding the self, or getting back to the self," or changing the unhealthy or neurotic behaviors that have hidden or taken us away from our "core self." Although existentialists are quite clear in their (our) belief in "existence precedes essence" (e.g. existence comes first, *who* we are, is constantly being created anew from moment to moment), it is still common for writers and practitioners to speak of the "self" as if it is this constant, unchanging entity. Again, borrowing from the Zen perspective, which sees the self as an illusion (e.g., not static but fluid and constantly changing), I prefer to utilize the concept of "potentiality" in lieu of "self." In Buddhism, we talk of the "no self" as a way to let go of the ego's desire to believe it is bounded (Epstein, 1995; Frager & Fadiman, 2005; Goleman, 1988). Thus like the metaphor of the onion where as we peel back layer by layer, we come to its center (where there is nothing, yet it is still an onion), Contextual Existential theory sees the process of therapy as uncovering, or remembering our "potentiality." It is the concept of potentiality (defined as the inherent capacity to come into being) that speaks to our unending ability to create and re-create who we are in the world. In this sense, existence *does* precede essence. The root of the word "existence" is "ex sistere," which is Latin for "to stand out, or to emerge." To move to our center is to remember our potentiality. By tapping into this potential "to be," we create and re-create our essence.

## The Role of Culture

Finally, and most importantly, Contextual Existentialism understands the crucial role that culture plays in the development of the individual (thus one reason for the term *contextual*). Without an understanding of and sensitivity to the myriad cultural factors that are at play in any given human being, we are prone to generalizations and stereotypical assumptions, or worse yet to completely interpreting behaviors and problems from the dominant cultural biases that influence our world-view. Psychology historically has interpreted human experience through a white, middle to upper class, heterosexual male perspective. Although in-roads are being made here with the influence of both feminist and multicultural psychological perspectives, contemporary theories still tend towards the old biases. Contextual Existentialism requires one to consider context at all times, to utilize tools such as a more formal cultural assessment (see Hays, 2001) in order to allow for understanding that furthers the potential for culturally sensitive and appropriate therapy.

## Contextual Existentialism Defined

Having explored both the historical nature of existential theory in general, and the areas that I feel have not been addressed or have been under-addressed, let us come to some understanding of what Contextual Existentialism is. While adhering to the core tenets of existential psychology and theory, Contextual Existentialism attempts to more clearly define and operationalize these concepts in an ever-changing, ever-evolving world. Through our understanding of the crucial roles that society and culture play in human development, Contextual Existentialism sets forth the following beliefs:

1. Human beings are whole and healthy, have the capacity for self-awareness, and the ability to access this self-awareness to move towards living authentic and congruent lives. Rather than using the concept of "self" which is most often interpreted as a static, unchanging entity, Contextual Existential theory utilizes the concept of "potentiality," which honors the understanding that we, in fact, are constantly creating and re-creating who we are in the world, "our essence."

2. The core motivation of human existence is to move toward balance (and homeostasis) between the mind, the body, the emotions, and the spirit, with an emphasis on integrating these four domains in a holistic and pro-active way.

3. Anxiety is a condition of living. It evidences itself in response to four basic givens of existence as human beings in this world: choice and responsibility, isolation and desire for connection, meaning and the experience of meaninglessness, awareness of death and non-being-ness and our striving for life. Healthy anxiety is a motivator for movement towards balance and authentic living. When avoided or denied, healthy anxiety becomes neurotic, creating a state of imbalance and in-

congruence.

4. Contextual Existentialism understands that human beings develop within a social and cultural context. These contextual relationships form deep and meaningful perspectives that influence how one experiences the world. In addition, relational and values development play crucial roles in the development of the healthy personality. Understanding primary relational styles learned during early childhood, and the levels of existence in relation to values development, are crucial to our understanding of how individuals deal with healthy and neurotic anxiety.

5. Living in the here and now is crucial to our ability to successfully transcend the moment and create our future. Through understanding the nature of paradox, the cultivation of mindfulness, the interconnectedness of all things, and the role of intuition, individuals can learn to utilize healthy anxiety as a motivating force in their lives.

6. Although an individually/intra-psychically focused theory, Contextual Existentialism, by its very nature, understands the relational nature of the world and thus can be utilized to understand and work with couples, families, and groups. In addition, it offers a way to understand larger social, cultural, educational, and organizational issues.

7. Contextual Existential theory avoids becoming technique focused, but rather sees (as does traditional existential theory) the therapist as the most powerful tool, and the therapeutic relationship as the primary healing mechanism. While healing occurs in the inter-subjective nature of relationship, assessment from a Contextual Existential perspective is seen as crucial to the therapist's ability to have a framework from which to operate, stressing the need to use this framework as a stepping off place to understand the issues while simultaneously letting go of this interpretation as the client allows his/her story to unfold. Assessment is thus a tool, not an answer, always leaving room for the client's meaning to lead the work. In addition, diagnosis is seen as a language that can be useful in consulting with colleagues about a client. As a language it can be useful in coming to some understanding of common themes in behavior across individuals (a phenomenological perspective), not as a prescription for rigid, dualistic ways of thinking about intervention. At its best, diagnosis is a-theoretical in nature, and allows room for a variety of theoretical interpretations and courses of action.

# II

# The Nature of Paradox

"How shall I grasp it? Do not grasp it. That which remains when there is no
more grasping is the Self."—Panchadasi

One of the foundations of existential psychology is the understanding that
although the subjective experience is highly valued as the most important route
to understanding experience, even the concepts of *subjectivity* and *objectivity*
represent a dualistic way of thinking. Existentialism has attempted to delve beneath this dualistic notion and find language and an understanding of what con-
tains these concepts. The notion of *paradox* is often used to explore this, with an
understanding that paradoxical thinking (and paradoxical experience) allows for
a both/and perspective. It offers us the possibility to see that one's subjective
experience of any given situation is by its very nature, real.

While existential theory holds the concept of paradox as central, and in this
way is a unique perspective in western psychological approaches, the literature
to date has not done much more than refer to it as a concept. It has become a
given within this theoretical framework, yet I believe having a deeper understanding of the experience of paradox makes it more useful. For this, I turn to
my experience and understanding of Zen Buddhist philosophy (Benoit, 1990;
Hirai, 1989; Kabat-Zinn, 1994; Suzuki, 1964). Like other avenues of Buddhist
thought, Zen Buddhism takes for granted the paradoxical nature of the world.
There is no right or wrong answer to any question, but rather multiple perspectives that allow us to come to a multitude of possible answers. This experience
of multiplicity leads us (quite naturally) to anxiety. From a Buddhist psychological perspective, if we choose to ignore or deny the anxiety, we lose our ability to see clearly, and we move out of our ability to be in the moment. We often
turn towards behaviors that keep us in avoidance or denial and cause dysfunctional patterns to emerge. From this Buddhist perspective these behaviors include addictions, delusions, and aversions (Frager & Fadiman, 2005). Addictions speak to anything that becomes a means to avoid one's experience of

living in the world. Not limited to drugs or alcohol, one can be addicted to material goods, money, a job, relationships, and a myriad of other possibilities. Delusions, although a cousin to the western pathological understanding of a psychotic symptom, is any cognitive process whereby an individual distorts the perception of their experience in order to avoid facing their own reality. Aversions are behaviors that allow someone to avoid uncomfortable situations, feelings or knowledge.

Connected to these avoidance mechanisms is the important Buddhist concept of non-attachment. While most often discussed in relationship to the western construct of ego, non-attachment is encouraged as a way to be fully present and aware, letting go not only of the illusion that we have some core "self" or identity, but also of any way of thinking, behaving, or feeling that moves us away from what is occurring from moment to moment. Thus addictions, delusions, and aversions all arise from attachment to a belief, an outcome, or perception of oneself that is most often static and entrenched.

# Ronnie

I had a client several years ago whom I will call Ronnie, who had been victimized by her father during her childhood. This incestuous relationship had lasted for several years, and often in the presence of her younger sister. This breach of trust on the part of the one man she should have been able to fully trust to protect her, altered her experience of both herself and the world for many years to come. When I first started seeing her, she was in her late twenties, and had been to two therapists before me. While there is no doubt in my mind that these other clinicians had honored her experience and offered support and guidance in her healing process, what also became clear is that she still maintained a perception of herself (and thus an identity) as "the victim." Whether it was because her previous therapists did not challenge this identity in her adult life, or because she was not yet ready to give it up, the bottom line is that she still lived her life as if she was still being abused.

Her helplessness, hopelessness, and anger not withstanding, Ronnie continued to live in the past, thus coloring any present moment experience with her history. In almost every relationship that had any depth, both with men and with women, Ronnie gave all responsibility to the other, then quietly fumed for not being seen and heard, or acted in passive-aggressive ways in order to sabotage the potential for a healthy connection. Her attachment to the belief and identity of herself as "victim" was so entrenched that she was unable to detach from it to see her own potentiality. Her belief that this was *who she is* did not allow for any other way of being.

As I worked with Ronnie, I focused her on her here-and-now experience of being in the room with me. I pushed her to stay aware of all of her experience, her feelings, her body, her thoughts and beliefs as we sat together. We often meditated together (early on she was only able to tolerate this space of self-awareness for brief periods) in order to bring her here-and-now experience of herself into focus. We explored the paradoxical nature of experience and the world. Over time she was able to be more comfortable with this, and began to see how the negative messages she had internalized from her father became the root of her self-perception. Because her father happened to be a minister in a fundamentalist church, we even used the metaphor of exorcism within several sessions to "purge" herself of her father's voice (and thus messages). More importantly, she became aware that although she had been victimized in her past, and her feelings about that experience were valid and important to honor, it was not *who she is now*. It did not define her from moment to moment; rather she could choose who she wanted to be from that moment on.

As Ronnie became more and more comfortable with being present, her sense of her potentialities grew. Her helplessness and hopelessness transformed into a sense of her power and capacity for life. Her anger and pain, while acknowledged, no longer was the driving force in her choice making. As she made meaning from her experience, her beliefs and values changed. In short, she began to live a more authentic life, and while not always peaceful and happy, she reported experiencing herself as "alive." Ronnie keeps in touch every now and then. Although she moved away to another city, she has been involved in a healthy and productive relationship and continues her process of growth and healing.

I share this story as a bridge to connect the Buddhist concepts of paradox and non-attachment to western existential beliefs; you can see many similarities, albeit with some different language. Yet what Zen offers us that is different, is a more specific way into understanding the paradoxical experience itself. Through the use of strategies like meditation and the cultivation of mindfulness, one can come to experience paradox in a different way that allows us to see the futility of avoiding our natural anxiety. It also helps us to see anxiety as part of our world, not to be frightened of, but rather to be embraced. Some of these ideas have been utilized in western existential practice, like the focusing technique offered by Eugene Gendlin (1981). Through a series of inwardly focused questions, one is lead to identify what might be at the core of his/her problems. Other forms of visualization work also are aimed at helping us to focus inwardly in order to identify areas of our life or past experiences that might have relevance in the work we are doing therapeutically. What is different here is that these interventions, while they can help us get to information, do not always work well in helping us learn how to really experience our anxiety in such a way that we can be-friend it. The intent is still towards alleviating it from our experience.

Now I know there will be those in the field who will argue vehemently against this premise, yet I see these interventions as coming very much from our western "do it" mentality, and as such not allowing us to move beneath this subjective/objective duality that we strive toward. While I recognize that as westerners, we are always going to see things with a certain bias, nonetheless I believe we are doing ourselves an injustice not to attempt to move deeper into our being-ness. By utilizing methods that allow us to move deeper, without necessarily expectations of an answer, we can begin to understand the paradoxical nature of anxiety itself. It is living the paradox that will teach us how to be in our lives more fully. By both wanting to find the answer, and simultaneously letting go of the expectation that we will find it, we can experience ourselves fully, and in the moment.

Think of anxiety as our beacon of light that warns us we are approaching a decision point. How we choose to choose ultimately moves us forward in our lives. Choosing not to choose is of course one possibility, unfortunately one that more often than not leads us to experiencing stuckness, and thus more anxiety. When we focus on the stuckness, the anxiety itself often becomes the focus of our world, thus neurotic in nature. We begin a vicious cycle of avoiding or denying the anxiety we are experiencing, and then, in turn, seeing the anxiety itself as the problem. This leads to all sorts of potential problems and behaviors which might include severe forms of anxiety, depression, psychosis, and the development of unhealthy personality traits. We must learn to move into the anxiety, to allow ourselves to experience it in its fullness, with a trust that by doing so, we will move forward and come to clarity with whatever the situation is that demands us to choose.

# Multiplicity

Since we understand that each individual is unique and thus will experience their world in a completely unique way, we also have to agree that our individual experiences, even of the same phenomenon, will result in unique perceptions and responses. This refers to the concept of *multiplicity*, a concept I believe is crucial to understand in order to become comfortable with paradox itself.

An example that demonstrates multiplicity might be to consider how you and your friends respond to a movie that you have seen together. With an understanding that you all sat down and experienced this movie in the same environment (the theater), at the same day and time, one might presuppose that your experiences would be the same. However, you each bring different backgrounds (social and cultural contexts), intra-psychic experience (your present feelings, thoughts, bodily sensations, value systems), and your interpersonal relational styles (ways in which you have learned to interact and interpret relationships). These unique contributions to who you are (and there are many more that we could discuss) will play a role in how you experience this film in the here and now. As you leave the theater to have coffee and discuss the film, undoubtedly you will have some similar responses. Yet as you take the discussion to a deeper, and perhaps more refined place, you will begin to uncover some differences. These might include emotional responses to all or parts of the film, or to specific characters. They might also include perceptions or interpretations of a characters motivation, or the director's intent. From an existential perspective, we would look at these differences and see them all as "true." How can we argue that your individual response is "false" and someone else's is "true"? Even if we

were to sit down with the director and ask his/her intent in filming a certain se-
quence in a certain way, does that take away the "truth" of your experience and
perception? What I am getting at here is the importance of acknowledging the
power of subjective experience as it forms meaning in one's life, yet at the same
time not negating the power of your friends very real but different experience of
the same event!

What happens then, internally, when you are confronted with this multiplicity of responses, each of which is "true" for the individual reporting it? You
could continue to argue for the "right" answer however more than likely this
would lead to power struggles and perhaps compromised friendships. You could
agree to disagree; actually a good solution, especially if in doing so you can acknowledge (at least to yourself) that there might not be any one "right" answer.
This then would be evidence of paradoxical thinking. Paradoxical *thinking* is
usually easier to deal with, as it often involves one's ability to hold more than
one "truth," most of which emanate from external sources (i.e., your friends' interpretations of the movie along with your own). However, paradoxical *experience* is an internal, intra-psychic event, and as such raises the bar on the anxiety
response. When anxiety is internally driven, it is usually experienced as more
difficult to navigate. Holding more than one "truth" in this way creates internal
conflict and pushes us toward some decision point. Allowing ourselves to sit
with this anxiety, rather than avoid or deny it, opens the door to ways in which
we can choose to live our lives authentically and congruently. This very real experience of anxiety arises from four paradoxes that existentialists believe are inherent conditions of living as human beings in the world—conditions that cross
cultures and experiences, perhaps at that level that Jung referred to as the collective unconscious.

# The Existential Paradoxes

Although existential psychology has intentionally attempted to not pigeon-
hole itself through a formal or rigid structuring of concepts and techniques,
when reviewing the writing of the major contributors to this theory, one sees
certain repeated themes emerge. One of these themes is the identification of the
four main "conditions of living" that are seen as at the core of the existential
struggle between individuals and living in the world. Although different writ-
ers/practitioners tended to focus more specifically on one or two of these conditions, there is general agreement that all four are present and active in our lives.
Yalom (1980) in particular, brought all four to the forefront of his work, with
detailed attention to ways in which they presented themselves in client's lives,
and more tellingly, the ways in which, through the avoidance of the anxiety they
produce, clients developed unhealthy responses. From a Contextual Existential
frame, I propose that it is essential to understand and assess how all four of these
conditions may be at play in any given clinical scenario in order to provide the
most useful therapeutic healing. Furthermore, by intentionally identifying them

as Existential Paradoxes, we more clearly can see their paradoxical nature, and more clearly understand the role they play in both producing anxiety and offering numerous possibilities for transcending it.

## Choice (Freedom) and Responsibility

This paradox recognizes the tension between our natural desires to be free, to create our own lives, our own futures; it is the recognition, often at a deep out of conscious awareness, that we are ultimately responsible for the consequences of our choices. This freedom, our ability to make choices, is intimately tied to responsibility. Understanding the concept of destiny is also important. From an existential perspective, destiny includes those factors in our lives that we have no control over: our biology (including genetics, abilities, race/ethnicity's, etc.) and the time and place into which we were born and raised, including events outside of our individual control. Yet even with destiny in mind, choice making is always available. As Frankl (1959/1984) so eloquently expressed it, even in the worst of conditions, even with those aspects that are out of our direct control, we still can choose our attitude and responses to our lives and those around us.

Realizing the both/and of this paradox creates anxiety, whether we are coming to this understanding consciously or not. As a result, we begin our struggle with this tension immediately by choosing to both allow ourselves to experience and learn from this anxiety or to deny or avoid it. In doing the latter, we repress the anxiety and as a result think, feel, and act in ways that support this avoidance. This leads to our movement out of balance, and the resultant unhealthy ways in which we interact with our world. We create neurotic anxiety, that is to say, anxiety that overwhelms us, becomes the center of our universe despite (and paradoxically due to) our desire to avoid it.

While all four paradoxes impact all realms of our lives (our inner intra-psychic world, our relational world, our natural world, and our spiritual world), this paradox usually evidences itself in intra-psychic (our inner world) ways more than any other. Specific kinds of behaviors that arise from our avoidance of this paradox include both compulsive and impulsive behaviors, such as those behaviors that we feel "compelled" to do (with full cognition) and/or "impelled" to do (outside of our consciousness, thus they feel automatic and spontaneous) (Yalom, 1980). Rationalization and projection are also common defensive strategies stemming from this "freedom anxiety." In these cases there is often a displacement of responsibility onto others or a denial of responsibility on our part. Finally, symptoms can also look like an inability to make a decision; what Yalom refers to as "decisional pathology," or a de-valuing of the decision/choice that is made.

## Isolation and Desire for Connection

This paradox explores the tension and resultant anxiety that arises from our deep awareness of our uniqueness (thus the understanding that we are truly alone in the world) and our innate desire to be connected in relationship to others. When we come to this realization, conscious or not, that there is no "other" in our world who can truly understand what it means to be "me," to truly grasp our experience of being in the world, we look to connection, to relationship with an "other" to ease the anxiety. In natural balance, we can hold this tension, yes, and even utilize it to empower ourselves as individuals, thus to use this core sense of whole self to make connection to others in healthy ways.

This paradox tends to have a major impact on our relational world. Specifically, the kinds of unhealthy responses that arise from avoiding the anxiety of this tension includes relational styles (compliant, detached, aggressive) (Horney, 1945), fusion/enmeshment in relationships with others or causes, using others to enhance one's own sense of importance or belonging, and the use of sex as a way to connect but without intimacy (Yalom, 1980) .

From a Contextual Existential perspective, I would also posit that this "desire to connect" includes not only connection to other human beings, but also to our natural world and to our spiritual (or meaning making) world. In turn, the kind of unhealthy responses that can arise from this paradox include those that reflect our perceived inability to connect to these arenas of our lives. As such, the impact is not only on our relational world, but on our natural and spiritual worlds also. More than the other three paradoxes, the role of society and culture have important roles to play in our understanding of one's individual and relational experience. One could argue that this paradox reflects the systemic nature of our world in the most profound ways, and as a result, we must always attend to the systemic implications within any given clinical situation.

## Death/Non-Being and the Striving for Life

While in many ways the "deepest" and often most difficult paradox to work with, nonetheless, this paradox also holds some of the most profound implications for healing. Seen as a paradox that works at both the concrete and metaphorical levels, this tension is between one's realization of our mortality (in the concrete) and the parallel struggle to live our lives fully and authentically. As we come to the awareness that our physical life is terminal and that there is no built-in program that tells us when we will die (thus one can see the attractiveness of suicide as one way to deal with controlling this anxiety), our innate tendency is to make the most of our lives. However, the anxiety that arises in this paradox often (quickly) moves this death awareness out of our consciousness. We experience death (and culturally have chosen to deal with it) as a dark, unspeakable image that is somehow a crime against humanity. This pushing away, both individually and culturally has had profound implications in our lives and our development as human beings.

In addition, and often parallel to this tension, is the metaphorical way in which we "die." That is to say, when our intrinsic wholeness has been ignored, denied or called in to question, especially during our formative years, we come to a false belief (often fostered by familial and social forces) that we have no real potentiality, or at best, a damaged one. Built upon a foundation of false-hoods, this "no self" or lack of ability to experience our innate potentiality, comes to hold a central role in our belief system; it thus affects most all aspects of our lives. When pushed by the healthy anxiety that arises from this paradox, we experience our selves as a "black hole" or "void," thus incapable of surviving any reflection or search for our "true self," our infinite potential. This meta-phorical struggle is between our innate desire to live our lives fully (to live from our whole center) and the belief that we have no center (therefore are already dead for all intent and purpose, and any reflective search will annihilate what-ever is left of us).

This paradox, while again having an impact on all levels of our existence, most profoundly affects our natural world (at the concrete level) and our intra-psychic world (particularly at the metaphorical level). Examples of how these result in certain unhealthy responses include magical thinking and/or more seri-ous psychotic symptoms, depression, enmeshment (merging with another keeps us from separate annihilation), and masochism (Becker, 1973; Yalom, 1980).

## Meaning and Meaninglessness

This final paradox represents the tension and resultant anxiety that comes from our growing awareness of the struggle between finding and creating mean-ing for ourselves in a world that often feels meaningless, and/or where meaning and values (one can discuss morals as a subset of values) are often prescribed from an outside source (family, society, religion, politics), yet might not reso-nate with our own internal frame of reference or intuitive knowledge. While re-cognizing that external structures for values are important in any social and cul-tural context (after all, we are relational beings, and living as part of a group or community means thinking not only of oneself, but of others), we still must struggle with how we develop individual understandings of values and ethics and belief systems. These meaning-making processes are inherent in our lives and development as healthy individuals living in a relational world. Yet we of-ten feel compelled, either overtly or covertly to accept the status quo. I would argue here that this essential developmental process is what helps hold the ten-sion (and thus holds the balance) between being an individual and being part of a group. It has strong connections to our struggle with isolation and connection.

This paradox, while having important relational connotations, most notably affects our spiritual (or meaning-making) world, that is to say, the world of val-ues, ethics and belief systems, which guide us in our understanding of our place, not only in the relational and natural world, but also in the larger universe. When we are in avoidance of the anxiety that arises from this paradox, responses in-clude apathy, boredom, a sense of emptiness, neurotic behaviors (depression, substance abuse, obsession, delinquency, risk-taking, hyper-inflation of sex), crusadism, nihilism, and compulsive activity (Yalom, 1980).

# Avoidance of the Moment

In both Existential and Zen Buddhist philosophies, attention to the here-and-now moment is of paramount importance. The belief that we are constantly creating and re-creating ourselves, and that "reality" can only be understood in the context of the present, guide us to understand that who we are and who can become are driven, in no small part, by the choices we make every second of our lives. We are both our history and our future, but only as it is lived in this moment. When we let our history or our future define us (as Ronnie did in my discussion earlier in this chapter), we have stopped living and creating ourselves; and more importantly, have chosen to believe that who we are is defined somehow in the external rather than internal world of experience. It is by being in the present moment, and choosing to live authentically, that we come to understand ourselves holistically, and can tap into that center that allows for creating meaning, relationship, and freedom within a fully lived experience. By attempting to ignore and/or deny the healthy anxiety that arises as a result of our awareness of the four existential paradoxes discussed above, we choose a focus on our past or a projection into the future, neither action allowing us to experience our present moment. By living our lives through the lenses of "if only I hadn't done/thought/been . . . " or "When I . . . ", we miss out on the opportunities that present themselves to us in the "now" of our experience. It is these opportunities to experience the natural anxiety of the unknown that allow us to transcend the moment and create our future. By effectively "choosing not to choose" we doom ourselves to a life lived through us, rather than being the architects of our life.

# III

# The Contextual Development
# of the Individual

"If you are lonely when you're alone, you are in bad company."
–Jean-Paul Sartre


Traditional existential writings offered the groundwork for understanding the phenomenological experience of individuals living in the world (Husserl, 1931; Kockelmans, 1967). Having a phenomenological focus gave greater flexibility for practitioners to consider the multiple factors that might need to be considered when working with a client. It opened the door, but in my belief, it did not do a very good job of exploring more fully the cross-cultural implications. Although one of the few psychological approaches included women's voices and discussed similarities with beliefs (specifically in the power of subjectivity and paradox) from other cultures, there was still a strong reliance on the white, male perspective. More importantly perhaps was the out-of-balance tendency to speak to the commonalties of the human experience without enough attention to considering (and supporting) the differences that come specifically from the role of culture in our lives. More recently, writers such as Clement Vontross (1979, 1999) have challenged practitioners to consider cultural factors in existential work; and in the process have offered larger constructs for considering such influences in our lives and how these might impact therapeutic work. I would argue, however, that more practical tools for both assessment and treatment are missing.

Contextual Existentialism believes that it is imperative to consider the context within which individuals are born, live and learn if one is to have a more complete understanding of their experiences. This in turn allows the clinician to offer a more useful therapeutic process. Rooted in the core beliefs of existential theory, that we are all healthy and unique, *and* we are in constant relationship with others and our world, this contextual understanding is critical in becoming culturally sensitive practitioners. Utilizing a Contextual Existential framework, therefore, incorporates a strong value in attending to assessing and responding to cultural factors in the make-up of each individual. It is also important to recognize both the effect of society and culture on the individual as well as the unique individual ways in which each person experiences and interprets their world. Thus, Contextual Existentialism cautions us to not generalize (and risk stereotyping) cultural factors in our work, but rather pro-actively learn about cultures different from ourselves, while still holding the experience and story of each person as unique. As a theoretical and clinical approach, it also goes one step further in offering some practical ways to implement this exploration, especially in how a clinician can consider multiple contextual factors in our attempts to understand our clients and their concerns. One way to better understand this is to first understand how we define "culture," and then to see that each of us, in all actuality, is influenced by a variety of cultures in both our inter-personal and intra-personal experiences.

## The Nature of Culture

Within the contextual frame, culture is defined fairly broadly. It includes not only race and ethnicity, but also recognition that issues of class, gender, sexual orientation, age, ability, and religion or spiritual values all have implications in how we come to know our world and ourselves. It is useful to turn to the multicultural literature to find a variety of perspectives on multicultural counseling and therapy. I have found the work of Hays (2001) and her ADDRESSING model to be the most valuable both in understanding the role of culture as well as in assessment. In this model, she provides a clear and straightforward methodology for considering the multiple cultural factors that contribute to one's experience. The acronym speaks to:

**A**ge and generational influences
**D**evelopmental disabilities
**D**isabilities acquired later in life
**R**eligion and spiritual orientation
**E**thnic and racial identity
**S**ocioeconomic status
**S**exual orientation
**I**ndigenous heritage
**N**ational origin
**G**ender (Hays, 2001, p. 18)

By using this cultural assessment model, clinicians can more accurately attend to both understanding and treating client's from a diversity of backgrounds and experiences. In addition, it provides a wonderful and often-overlooked emphasis on exploring the clinician's own cultural context. I will utilize this model combined with the Contextual Existential focus on foreground and background, within more specific clinical examples in later chapters.

Keeping in mind that this theory always is utilizing a social and cultural lens with which to view human beings, I would like to address the role of relational development and of values development. The remainder of this chapter focuses on two specific areas that Contextual Existentialism offers as ways to understand the role of development in the individual.

## Relational Development

Embedded deeply within existentialism is the paradox of isolation and connection. It is understood that as human beings, we respond to our awareness of our ultimate aloneness in the world; although others are around us, and we were each born from our mother's womb, nonetheless we are unique and our experiences of being in the world are not ever fully shared with anyone else. This deeply felt knowledge of our aloneness pushes us to attempt to make contact with others, to find a way to share our lives and experiences, to be seen. From a Contextual Existential perspective, even more importantly, we come to know ourselves by our relationship with others and our world. But, how do we connect to others? Besides understanding this as an existential drive, why do we relate to others in the ways that we do? What is healthy and what is not? I turn to the work of Karen Horney (1945/1972) to help elucidate the process by which we develop our relational self.

Karen Horney, although psychoanalytically trained, is known as one of the earlier humanists, as well as a formidable feminist voice within the psychological community. Her parallel work to the early Object-Relations theorists, while sharing an agreement on the importance of early childhood experiences of attachment and separation, moved beyond them with her clear understanding of the white male biases inherent in her colleagues' theories, both in terms of the impact on women, but also of the impact on men. Beyond this, she spoke of the need to understand the role of culture in how human beings develop and come to understand themselves and their world. Influenced by the social nature of Adler's work (1927/1992), and the humanistic nature of the work of Fromm (1949/1964, 1956/2000), Horney recognized that safety and trust were crucial to how children developed their relational selves. Of most interest to the contextual existential frame, is her work on identifying the ways in which early childhood caregiving affected how infants and children came to respond to others and their world. It was understood, as in other analytic theories that this process happened most naturally between the ages of six months and two years.

Not unlike the Object-Relations theorists, she posited that caregivers, being the imperfect human beings that they are, most often are unable to provide an equally balanced pattern of attention and withdrawal, so necessary for children to feel safe enough to begin their separation process. This pattern of connection and disconnection is a natural dance that all young children go through in order to become more fully aware of themselves as unique individuals while still feeling part of a community. What usually happens, however, is that children experience caregivers who err on the side of too much attention or too much withdrawal; or in more severe cases, the product becomes one of enmeshment or neglect. In any case, children in these situations, naturally respond to the subtle or not so subtle ways in which they experience this over-protection or neglect, with subtle or not so subtle responses. As noted in Chapter 1, Horney (1945/1972) named these relational styles as *compulsive compliance, compulsive detachment*, and *compulsive aggression*. Any of these styles of relating could arise out of either over-protective or neglective stances of the primary caregivers. Let me give some examples:

An infant/child experiences an over-protective caregiver. The experience of the child is one of being overwhelmed, of being smothered, of losing any sense of their burgeoning "potentiality." This child might respond in one of three ways in order to preserve his/her sense of a center, or in existential terms, to preserve homeostasis. One possibility is to become compliant. If I could put words into this child's head, they might be, "If I'm really good, and do whatever it is s/he wants me to do, maybe s/he will leave me alone." A second stance might be to detach. Again, the words might be, "I'm feeling smothered, I can't escape! Nothing I seem to do works, so I'll just act as if it doesn't matter. If I'm indifferent, maybe I'll be left alone!" The third approach might be to become aggressive, to push against. Here, the child might be thinking, "I keep trying to get you to leave me alone, but you don't get it! Maybe I need to become defiant, to yell and scream or push and shove! Then maybe, you'll leave me alone!"

On the other hand, if the infant/child is responding to an experience of neglect, of not being seen and/or heard, all three of these same stances might still be in operation. The difference is that the motivating factor comes from neglect rather than enmeshment. Thus the inner voice of the child will sound a little different. For the child who compensates through compliance, we might hear, "If I'm really good, and do everything you want me to do, maybe you'll pay attention to me, and you'll see me!" For the detached child, the message is, "It hurts so much when you don't see or hear me, so to deny the hurt and anger for your ignoring me I'll come to believe that I don't need you anyway. I don't need anyone! If I don't need you, then I won't be hurt again." Finally, for the aggressive response, we might hear (probably with a shout), "Hello! I'm here! Why aren't you paying attention to me! Fine! I'll make you pay attention to me. I'll scream and yell and act out until you do! Negative attention is better than none at all!"

As you can see, whether or not the infant is over-protected or ignored, the three relational styles work pretty well as a compensation mechanism. In both analytic and existential terms, these ways of coping set up an image and belief about the world and about him/herself that leads the child to respond in almost any situation in the same relational way. The more profound the experience of enmeshment or neglect, the more rigidly the child utilizes this way of coping in relationship. It, in effect, becomes her/his predominant style of relating, not only to other human beings, but also to the world itself. The persistent lack of safety and trust at such an early age transfers itself to a world view, and lays the ground for a whole array of defense mechanisms to be utilized in order to create a sense of safety and trust. And, without appropriate intervention, or a change in the way the child experiences his/her world of relations, this becomes the modus operandi for her/him, as s/he grows into adulthood. In addition, through both over-protection and/or neglect, the child is unable to learn how to respond to the natural, existential anxiety that arises as a result of the isolation/striving for connection paradox. So much time and attention (and energy) is going towards learning how to cope with lack of safety and trust, there is no room for the emergence of the healthy developmental aspect of not only this, but all of the paradoxes of our existence.

In the healthy process of growth and development in relationship, a child can learn to choose among all three relational styles dependent upon the very real circumstances that they encounter. In fact, to be able to move freely between being compliant, detached, or aggressive is a sign of healthy relational development, because the world and many people in it are not always safe. When this natural and healthy connection/separation process is compromised, all sorts of unhealthy patterns are established, all of which can have an impact on how the individual deals with the paradoxes of existence. This is because the child has learned how to not trust the here-and-now experience of their world, nor the inherently healthy and whole being-ness of their existence. This relational adaptation has led them to forget what they know, and to constantly need to be hypersensitive to their surroundings, thus living in the past or the future, rather than the present. Fortunately, Horney, as with existential theory, believes in the always-present opportunity to grow, heal, and change. Existential theory adds to this the unconditional belief in the natural proclivity of humans to seek health and balance.

# Lonesome Sam

Sam came to see me when he was 42 years old. He complained of a history of depression, lasting most of his adolescent and adult life, although he reported no times of severe depressive episodes. He was always able to maintain work, and his social life was described as adequate, although he had never really had a long-time, intimate relationship. Sam was born to a drug-addicted mother, although she somehow managed to not use during most of her pregnancy, including the critical early trimester. Upon his birth, however, she returned to using. His father did not use, nor had a history of use. Sam is mixed race, White and Cherokee Indian. He spent the early part of his life on the reservation, leaving with his father when his father got a job in the city.

During his first two years, his mother was his primary caregiver, but due to her use of drugs, he was often left alone in his crib, or later in a playpen, not receiving much attention from her. At times she would forget to feed or change him. Clearly this could be seen as physical abuse through neglect, but to her credit, she never hit him, nor did she ever leave him alone physically, although she was often not emotionally or mentally present when she was high. Even when sober, she did not provide the kind of consistent emotional and physical care necessary for healthy development. Since his father was at work, this left little Sam without much attention. Despite being on the reservation where "family" is really the entire community, his mother tended to isolate and not accept the support that the community offered. Sam's response to this neglect was to detach. One could say that somewhere in his still forming mind, he chose to "go away" rather than deal with this lack of attention and care. Fortunately for Sam, when his father was home after work, he provided the kind of attention that Sam so sorely needed, thus providing some context for relational development that proved immensely important as Sam grew up. Nonetheless, Sam had learned to detach as a way of coping, and although his father left his mother when Sam was three, her lack of care instilled in Sam a defensive posture that continued to permeate his life. Even with a healthier environment with his father as he grew into later childhood and adolescence, his dad still needed to work, and Sam was left in daycare environments, or with neighbors. His detached style of relating helped him to deal with a continuous stream of experiences where he felt abandoned and alone.

This detached relational style served Sam well in his life. If he, at some level, believed that he did not need the attention and care of another, then he did not have to experience the angry and hurt feelings that were repressed out of his awareness. He became very self-sufficient, focusing most of his time on doing well academically, and on tasks that were done in isolation. During his childhood and early adolescence, this usually came in the form of model making, and reading. When he was old enough to work, he got a job after school and on weekends, which kept him occupied. His social life was limited to a handful of friends in school and at work. He described these as casual friendships, and avoided any attempts by others to get closer to him. On the rare occasions that he found himself attracted to a girl, if she indicated any desire to get closer, he found excuses to move away.

By the time Sam came to see me, he reported several years of increased depression, a desire for more intimate relationships, and intermittent experiences of anxiety, which left him incapacitated. It was these "anxiety attacks" as he called them that brought him to therapy. In the course of our work, it was not only important to carefully consider Sam's contextual experience (his cultural background, current experiences and beliefs), but to understand his relational style and how it served him, both historically and currently. In addition, I needed to have some understanding of how these experiences and approaches to life played out in relation to the paradoxes. It was my job to explore Sam's here-and-now experience in relation to these contextual existential concepts, and to fluidly assess and let go of my perceptions as Sam told his story from moment to moment, and session to session.

It seemed that Sam was struggling with the isolation and connection paradox. His "anxiety attacks" were his responses to his emerging desire to be connected more intimately while simultaneously beginning to feel his feelings of anger, grief, and fear that had been repressed for so many years (thus why he experienced depression). From a Contextual Existential perspective, these "anxiety attacks" were seen as signs of his healthy center pushing for balance in his life. His detached mode of relating was no longer serving him, and his natural desire to seek his potentiality was coming forth. On some level, he understood that it was safe for him to emerge and re-create himself. Rather than continue to live in his past, that is, to approach the world and others in it as unsafe and untrustworthy, Sam's natural striving for homeostasis moved him toward the healthy anxiety that is at the root of our existence. His attempts to avoid this anxiety resulted in a history of depression, and more recently, neurotic anxiety (the attacks). Even in our relationship, I needed to constantly push him to stay present and to be aware of how he attempted to detach from me in our work.

If we are to navigate our world, to respond effectively to the paradoxical nature of the givens of our existence, then we must understand how we have come to know ourselves as unique individuals and how we connect to others and the world around us. In a profound way, the concepts of the Umwelt (the biological world), the Mitwelt (the social world), the Eigenwelt (the self-world), and the Überwelt (the spiritual/meaning-making world) (Barrett, 1958; van Deurzen-Smith, 1988) all are dependent to some degree or the other, on how we deal with the Isolation-Connection paradox. We come to understand and experience our aloneness *because* of our connection to others (and vice versa), thus we come to respond to and act upon the natural, the social, the intra-psychic, and the spiritual domains of our world based upon our ability to face the anxiety that inevitably arises in those moments of awareness of self and other.

Finally, while holding our understanding of the relational styles outlined by Horney (1945/1972), and set within an existential understanding of isolation and connection, we must also attend to the varied cultural aspects of the client's experience. What are the cultural norms and beliefs about parenting? About language and communication? About roles and relationships? Through specific cultural lenses, what might compliant, detached, or aggressive behavior look like? What are the unique variations on these cultural concepts experienced by the individual him or herself? All of these questions and considerations are crucial to understanding through a Contextual Existential frame.

In Sam's case, I used our relationship as a template for Sam to begin to experience a safe and trusting connection, a place where he could be fully seen, heard and attended to without judgment. As he came to trust our relationship, he began to let himself experience his feelings more fully, to find that they would not overwhelm him. In addition, he was able to understand why his detached style had come about, and how it had served him so well early in his life. He began to make choices to connect to others and the world more intentionally, and over time, began to feel more fully alive and able to enter into friendships and eventually deeper relationships without losing himself. Critical to this work together, was my understanding of Sam's cultural background (his struggle with his biracial identity), and how he uniquely experienced himself within this context (his desire for community while simultaneously being afraid of intimacy). How Sam played out his detached relational style, while having some similarity to how others might experience it, also had many differences, thus our work looked different than it did when I worked with another client with a similar way of relating to the world.

# Values Development

Soren Kierkegaard's discussion of choice and responsibility has had a profound impact on the development of existentialism, especially the paradox of freedom and responsibility. According to Barrett (1958), Kierkegaard speaks to how human beings come to know "self" through choice making. "He encounters the Self that he is, not in the *detachment* of thought, but in the *involvement* and pathos of choice." (p. 163). He continues to elaborate by discussing three levels of existence, the aesthetic, the ethical, and the religious. These levels offer an understanding of how we come to make choices. While within a Contextual Existential frame we would substitute the word "self" for "potentiality," the concepts and understanding is still crucial to our work.

At the aesthetic level, one is spontaneous and living in the moment, thus choices are made from this place of spontaneity. This is very much how small children live in the world, living solely for the immediate pleasure. However, at some point, when pleasure is not experienced, one can be thrown quickly into despair. It becomes a growing awareness that we, in fact, are not the center of the universe. This moves us to the second level, that of the ethical. The ethical expands the circle to include the relational, both to others and the world around us. Choice making occurs here with an understanding that there are impacts of our decision making beyond our own experience. This, then, is the domain of rules and values that speak to how one is in relationship. Often these come from outside us, internalized from family, community, religion, politics, etc. Finally, there is the religious level. Here the circle expands even further to incorporate our ability to live in the world authentically. From this place, fraught with our existential angst, we make decisions that move us towards our authenticity, our center. Here is where we might make choices that are in seeming contradiction to the rules and values and norms that we have been taught. In Contextual Existentialism, I choose to call this last stage the religio-spiritual stage, to de-emphasize the traditional ways that the word "religious" is interpreted. Rather, I want to be more inclusive of the focus on our inherent spiritual nature that might include both dogmatic and non-dogmatic belief and value systems.

Kierkegaard (in Barrett, 1958) offered up these *levels of existence* to help us understand how to move closer to our center. He did not see them as hierarchical in nature, in the sense that one did not leave the aesthetic and ethical behind as you move towards the religious. Rather, he seems to describe a way of understanding the development of our choice-making capacities, a natural process that guides us in our inherent movement toward authentic living. I would posit that in a very clear way, Kierkegaard has offered a framework from which I have created a more formal developmental model that spells out a way in which we come to know ourselves through the development of our own moral and ethical code of living. Not unlike other developmental models that speak to sexual or social development, the *levels of existence* help us understand how naturally we move from the normal and healthy narcissistic experience of childhood, where we experience ourselves as the center of the universe, to the recognition in later childhood that we are part of a community of others living in relation to our natural world. Here we must understand that choices are made with respect to the "other," such that healthy choices can support our self in-relation. Finally, as we mature into adulthood and begin to come to some sense of our own beliefs and values, we begin to make choices that move us towards our authenticity, not in denial of self-in-relation, but also encompassing our connection with spirit.

In Contextual Existentialism I take Kierkegaard's ideas and more fully develop them into a values developmental model as another way of understanding how and why individuals make the choices they do, and how their experiences of suffering inhibit or guide their movement toward authenticity. I would also posit that, as with any developmental model, one can become "stuck" in a level, which has a major impact on how one makes choices, and how the outcome of that choice making inhibits homeostasis. Ultimately, when one is stuck at any level, they are outside of temporal reality. No longer is the past and future contained in the present moment, but rather the past, present, and future have become dis-connected. Although this provides some semblance of safety, it is temporary. It is a decision to choose not to choose.

When one is stuck at the aesthetic level, one is stuck in the present, but outside of time. In other words, there is no connection to past or future here, so that the present focus becomes static in and of itself, and the individual loses any ability to make decisions to transcend the moment, but rather decisions are made only to stay in this "stuckness." When one is stuck in the ethical level, one is stuck in the past or future, but unable to be in the present. All decisions seem to be either/or, right/wrong, good/bad. The individual has chosen dualism to avoid the anxiety of living in the world. The focus is external only, so that consequences can also be externalized and not owned. When one is stuck in the religio-spiritual, one is usually stuck in the future, although one can be stuck in the past as well. Decisions are made as a way to avoid the present, by abdicating all choice and responsibility to God, or some other spiritual power greater than oneself, or to a cause. Rather than choosing to transcend oneself in order to create one's future, transcendence is an attempt to leave the world completely, or at the least to avoid the anxiety of living in the world. It is important to know that often we are stuck between the aesthetic and ethical, or between the ethical and spiritual; unable to decide whether or not to risk transcending our moment and experiencing freedom.

Within the contextual existential frame, we must once again also take into consideration the role of culture. How do specific cultural groups define the role of the individual within the group/community? Especially at the ethical level, what are the group norms and values? What are the real and potential consequences, both to the individual and the group, when an individual chooses in apparent contradiction to the group?

Going back to Sam, he had managed to successfully transcend the natural narcissistic stage of his development despite his mother's neglect, most likely due to his healthier relationship with his father. In addition, he was raised in a culture that holds a significant value of the importance of group over the individual, thus how Sam played out his detached style of relating was still within the context of the group. He did not tend to see the world in dualistic ways, except perhaps in his view of relationships as most always unsafe. Where Sam got stuck was between the ethical and religio-spiritual levels. Because he spent so much of his life keeping himself safe and living in the past, he had no time or energy to focus on what were his own values and beliefs. It was easier to passively accept what the external world told him was important. Although he was not rigidly stuck in this ethical realm, he did not challenge himself to examine his own values and beliefs. It was not until he had come to understand his own history and relational style, and the impact this had on his life, that he began to question the domain of belief systems.

As he became more capable of living in the present and taking risks in his choices of connection, he also began to become less willing to accept what others told him to believe. Over time, he started to explore his beliefs and values, where they came from, and what he wanted to keep, discard, or revise. He reported this process as scary and exciting, but simultaneously also stated that he felt more alive than he had ever experienced before in his life.

# Summary

Contextual Existentialism puts forth a belief in the importance of understanding and assessing both the relational style and values development of the individual as part of the process of healing and growth. By integrating concepts set forth by Karen Horney (1945/1972) and Soren Kierkegaard (in Barrett, 1958), we can deepen our ability to work successfully with clients in facilitating their natural progression towards homeostasis. These specific frameworks for understanding human experience contribute to a larger contextual understanding of how we all struggle to make sense of the givens of our existence. As with all other tools for understanding within this theory, there is a need to use them as a frame of reference for understanding, not as a static answer to the problem. We must always be willing to let go of our perceptions when they do not fit for the client, or as the client (and their story) grows and changes. In future chapters, we will return to these concepts as we see other case examples of assessment and treatment within this theoretical approach.

# IV

# The Use of Intuition

"All credibility, all good conscience, all evidence of truth come only from the senses."—Frederich Nietzsche

Apart from the work of Bergson (2002) and Pascal (in Barrett, 1958), both of whom are at times (and dependent upon whom one reads) connected to the development of existential thought, there is little in the literature about the role of intuition in existential psychology. Even with these two contributors, the emphasis is on a discussion of intuition in relation to rationality and science, emphasizing the limitations of abstract intelligence in an understanding of the totality of human experience. It is not until the work of Moustakas (1990), where he utilizes the work of Polanyi (1969) in his development of the Heuristic Research methodology, do we come to a discussion of intuition as central to one's phenomenological experience of living in the world.

Moustakas (1994) draws on the works of Husserl (in Lauer, 1967; and Levinas, 1967) and defines intuition as a bridge between tacit knowing (knowledge without words) and our more intellectual understanding and ability to express our experience. Almost hidden in his treatise of heuristics, this concept leaps out to divulge an integral component to the ways in which we may come to understand not only "self" or "potentiality," but also "self-in-relation."

Contextual Existentialism embraces the notion of intuition and by the very nature of its relationship to tacit knowing, sees intuition as crucial in how we can guide our clients and ourselves towards a deeper understanding of our experiences. Furthermore, based on my own clinical experiences (both as therapist and client) for the past 20 plus years, I would put forth a further clarification and definition of intuition, which sees it not only as a process, but also as a core capacity for understanding that we each have within us. This core capacity for knowledge (most often non-verbal) I call the Intuitives, and see them as avenues for understanding that comes directly through our senses, most notably kinesthetic, auditory, and visual. I would argue, in fact, that each of us has a more highly developed sense that is our primary vehicle for intuitive knowledge, and that becoming aware of this, and strengthening it, allows us to work with and access knowledge within the client-therapist relationship that would otherwise go un-noticed.

I would like to be clear here, that in this discussion, I neither rule out the usefulness of the olfactory and/or gustatory senses, nor do I eliminate the concept of a sixth (or seventh or eighth) sense. Rather, I base this on my own experiences, thus my own understanding of work I have done with clients and as a supervisor of other therapists that has, over time, proven to be highly useful within the therapeutic relationship. My main digression from previously held definitions of intuition is twofold. First, that intuition is not *the* sixth sense, but rather shows itself through all of the senses; and secondly, it is not merely an abstract concept to describe knowledge outside of the intellect; but rather both a process and an inherent ability to deepen and clarify a way of knowing about our lived experiences in the world that can be brought more fully into awareness, thus utilized as a tool for growth and healing.

## The Intuitives and Homeostasis

We have come to understand through earlier discussions, of the role of homeostasis in the natural process of growth and healing in Contextual Existential thought. Since homeostasis is described as an integrative process to bring balance between the somatic, emotional, cognitive, and spiritual domains inherent within each human being, and we have come to see that for each of us, there is a tendency to over-rely on one (or maybe two) of these domains as a way to avoid our existential anxiety, the Intuitives provide a channel for identifying and naming the lived experience that is often un-named but present in the moment. For example, for someone who tends to be more in their "head" (the cognitive) at the expense, to some degree or another, of their emotions, body, and/or spirit, utilizing the therapist's intuitive to name what is un-named (but known at some level) can be useful in confronting this out-of-balance experience and bringing some awareness into the therapeutic process.

We understand from an existential perspective that there are always three forces in the room during a therapeutic encounter: the client, the therapist, and the relationship between them. It is by bridging the phenomenological experiences of the client and the therapist through this third force, the relationship, that the opportunity for healing and growth occurs. It is in the place where the "I" and "Thou" meets and connects, this inter-subjective space, that the possibilities for the future to unfold are held. To further clarify utilizing more traditional analytic language, that which is un-named (thus dis-owned) by the client is energetically "thrown" into the room, into this space between client and therapist, the therapeutic relationship. It is "transferred" through its dis-owning, to this central field of experience, thus accessible to the therapist as well. This transference is basically a statement by the client saying, "I don't want to know this, to hold this" and it is crucial that the therapist is able to recognize this, understand what is his/her experience and what belongs to the client, and to provide a safe container for the dis-owned energy to be held in the room, through the means of the therapeutic relationship. Again, this inter-subjective third force allows the knowledge to be seen and heard until the client is able to re-own it and integrate it back into their experience. Thus here, the therapist might name a feeling, a body sensation, or an image that they are experiencing as the client presents their story, throwing it back into the room, always with a willingness to let it go if the client does not connect (which may accurately reflect what is happening, or may speak more to a level of denial on the client's part, which is also useful information). More often than not, the client will recognize it as their own, suddenly making a connection that they previously would not have made, or were unaware of. Sometimes, it may also be the therapists own counter-transferential material, thus s/he must always be open to attending to this as well.

Unfortunately, in more traditional analytic and other psychodynamic approaches, this transferential experience is held on an intellectual level, and often translated and interpreted only by the therapist. In addition, when the therapist is unaware of her/his own intuitive process, and is more than likely relying on the cognitive (since that is what most western theories of psychology are built on), they are missing all sorts of information that the client is clearly sharing. They are also more prone, I believe, to counter-transference as a result. When not aware of his or her own non-cognitive experiences (or perhaps non-dominant intuitive experience), there is a higher risk of mis-identifying one's own response as a projection from the client, if noticed at all. Since we are all "imperfectly perfect," this unfortunate predicament moves the therapy out of the here-and-now, and usually results in a return to a dualistic way of exploring the therapeutic relationship. Even more unfortunate, is that the awareness of the client-in-relationship-to-therapist field of experience is lost.

In a Contextual Existential approach then, the identifying of and further training of the therapist's primary intuitive mode(s) are highly useful in both assessment and treatment of clients. Furthermore, because the use of the Intuitives as a therapeutic tool help keep the work in the here and now (since the transferential material erupts in the moment of contact between client and therapist), the naming of the dis-owned and thrown energy places it squarely into the relational field of the therapeutic encounter and allows for a safe, albeit not always comfortable, opportunity to explore the anxiety that underlies the symptoms, existential paradox, and out-of-balance domains of the clients in-the-world experience. Over time, the additional ability to guide the client into recognizing her/his own primary Intuitives and learning how to utilize them proactively and intentionally can increase the capacity for mindfulness and authentic choice making. Ultimately, since the dis-owned aspects of experience usually are evidence of those domains that are under-developed, the use of the Intuitives in the therapeutic process also serves as a vehicle for developing the client's under-utilized domains. This, in turn, begins the process of bringing balance back to the client's life. By normalizing our relationship to each of the four domains, we come to use them in healthier ways, thus being more aware of the choices we make and the impact of these choices on our ability to live our lives more fully.

# Gaby

Gaby was a 27-year-old Latina of Mexican and Caucasian heritage who I had seen for approximately 7 months. She came from a successful middle class family who has been in the U.S. for two generations. Her father's family is of German and Irish descent, her mother is from Mexican and German descent. She was raised Jewish, as this was the religion of her mother's family, although Gaby described her own relationship to this identity as more cultural than religious. Her mother, however, is deeply religious, as her family had been involved with a tightly knit Mexican Jewish community in Mexico City prior to her grandparent's emigration to the U.S. Her father's family is Catholic, but he agreed to have his children raised in the Jewish faith. Gaby is an elementary school teacher in her second year of teaching. She is heterosexual and has no stated disabilities. She came to see me upon recommendation of a friend who had suggested I might be able to help her with her experiences of anxiety and stress.

As we began to work together and Gaby's story unfolded, she reported that she had been having many somatic complaints that, when checked out by her doctor, showed nothing physically wrong. These included headaches, intestinal cramps, and occasional chest pains. As it turns out, she has experienced these symptoms on a few occasions since her late adolescence, but not to the degree that they have been happening over the past year and a half. She also reports that her job is highly stressful and she is experiencing a fair amount of job dissatisfaction, thus has been questioning her career choice. She teaches first and second graders, and reports large classes with several challenging kids, due to a mix of some behavioral problems and some cases of English being the second language. She feels that there is little support in the school for teachers except with each other, and as a beginning teacher, she often feels "hung out to dry." Her questioning of her career is painful for Gaby, as she feels strongly about her original passion of becoming a teacher, which propelled her through her graduate training.

As Gaby tells her story from session to session, I became aware of her pattern of intellectualizing her life and world experiences. It seemed clear to me that she was very comfortable in the cognitive, but I rarely saw or sensed any emotion. In addition, I was acutely aware that in session (as I suspect was the case in the rest of her life), when talking about difficult issues or situations, her body spoke volumes. Her breathing was most often from the chest rather than from the diaphragm, she would fidget in her chair, her posture would often close in, and she would often cross her arms and hands protectively over her chest and/or stomach. She rarely looked relaxed and comfortable unless she was talking about a neutral subject, someone else, or an experience that was positive.

When I would stop her and point out these somatic patterns, she was surprised and unaware of what she was doing. In fact, it was quite uncomfortable for her to "be seen" in this way.

Much of my initial work with Gaby was to draw her attention to what I was seeing and experiencing being with her in the room. In particular, I wanted to help her see that she was not in the here-and-now, and that the severity of her symptoms was one piece of evidence of this. There were many occasions where I too experienced myself breathing shallowly, or experiencing stomach, chest, and later on, neck and head pain while working with her. Most often, these experiences happened as Gaby would tell a story about her stress or frustration, again, most often without any emotion. Almost always, when I would stop her and share my experience of being with her, especially my own somatic experiences, she would realize that she was experiencing the same symptoms in the same physical place. As our work progressed, I soon began experiencing more feelings of anger and sadness, as her story would unfold. Her reactions to my sharing of these "symptoms" would be to physically tighten up even more. With further gentle pushing, asking her to breathe deeply and allow herself to experience the somatic symptoms rather than try to make them go away, she began to touch on the feelings underneath them; not surprisingly anger and sadness were not uncommon.

As Gaby began to allow herself to open up to more of her whole experience, she began to make connections between her history of emotionally disconnecting and the fact that in her household, dominated by her mother, any feelings outside of "happy" were not tolerated. In fact, she began having specific memories of her mother telling her that she was not feeling "anger" or "sadness" or "frustration" when, in fact, this is what she was feeling. She learned early on to shut down her emotions, even to the point of deadening her ability to feel real happiness and joy. This makes sense, because when we restrict our feelings on one end of the continuum, it will affect our ability to feel fully on the other end as well. A powerful recognition came with Gaby's realization that her mother experienced her life the same way, with little emotional connection. It was how she had learned how to survive in her life, and she had taught Gaby well.

The additional work that unfolded was how this disconnection from her wholeness, also diminished Gaby's sense of her own beliefs, values, and wishes and wants. While developmentally, Gaby was at an age where differentiating from familial and social/cultural "norms" is common, the lack of living in the here and now of her wholeness had cut her off from her own exploration of meaning in her life. She disclosed at one point that her mother had not been very supportive of her going into teaching, and thus her internal struggle with whether or not this was really her desired career choice had many implications, not the least of which was what her mother might say if Gaby were to leave teaching.

Gaby struggled with all of the existential paradoxes as we worked together, with issues of meaning and choice being in the forefront for most of our time. However, what is important in this particular case study, is the awareness of how I was able to utilize my own kinesthetic intuitive as a primary tool in our work, and that with these interventions, Gaby too, was able to begin to utilize her intuition to bring more balance to her domains, and a trust in her own capacity to make meaningful choices by attending to her whole experience from moment to moment. By the way, Gaby is still teaching. She (at least in this moment) believes that it is her calling. Her frustration is a valid one due less to her career, and more to the structure of the educational system she works for. This realization does not always take away her stress, but it does allow her to experience it for what it is, and to more easily move through it and let it go. She reports that her increasing awareness of her potentiality also has had an impact on her interactions with her students, stating that she is able to be more present for them, which often (but not always) results in a decrease in their own disruptive behavior.

## The Intuitives as a Mediator for Anxiety

We have seen how the use of the Intuitives can help identify and process client's imbalanced use of their cognitive, emotional, somatic, and spiritual domains, primarily through the naming and working through of their dis-owned experiences. I would further advocate that the Intuitives also are a way to understand and mediate the existential and/or neurotic anxiety that arises as a result of our awareness of the paradoxes of living. Obviously, all of these concepts and experiences are inter-connected, thus speaking to the paradoxes here is merely a way to examine and understand their effect in a more simplified manner. It by no means attempts to speak to anxiety and the paradoxes as if they were separate components of the human experience.

As discussed earlier in Chapter 2, the four elemental paradoxes of human existence portrayed through various existential writers, and further clarified by existential psychologists and analysts, include those of freedom (choice) and responsibility, isolation and desire for connection, meaning and meaninglessness, and death (non-being) and striving for life. When these paradoxes, which are always at play, enter into our awareness at whatever level, they produce existential anxiety. This anxiety, if experienced and utilized can guide us towards an opportunity to transcend the moment, and move us into our future. By ignoring or denying this anxiety, it becomes neurotic and static, and moves us out of our here-and-now experience, often freezing us into living in our past or projecting ourselves into our future with no grounding in the present. The farther out of our awareness these paradoxes are, the more likely we are to ignore or deny them, thus developing unhealthy responses to our in-the-world experiences.

Contextual Existentialism adds to this a more overt belief that the more our early childhood experience, particularly of connection and relating (both to others and our natural and universal world) is inhibited, the more difficult it is for us to respond to this healthy anxiety. In addition, within the context of our environment and culture, we have opportunities to create meaning (through values and belief systems), which lead us towards our abilities to make healthy choices.

If we are discouraged or inhibited from developing our meaning-making self, our choice-making potentialities are also inhibited, leading to a disruption of being-in-the-moment and contributing to the increase in neurotic anxiety as a result of making life-threatening rather than life-affirming choices.

When our experiences with making connection as a way to understand ourselves, and making meaning in order to understand our self-in-relation, are compromised, it affects our ability to work from our healthy center to make choices. We have a difficult time navigating the healthy anxiety that is present, thus often experience our center as a "black hole" that will annihilate us, rather than experiencing this space as full of potentialities. This then impedes our movement to transcend ourselves and create our future, and ultimately how we come to understand who we are and what our purpose is in our world, in order to live our lives fully and authentically in the face of our own mortality.

With these understandings, the Intuitives become a useful therapeutic tool for bringing to the forefront the anxiety being experienced by the client in the moment. Remember that anxiety can manifest in many ways, with any or all four of the domains contributing symptoms. Emotionally, we might experience fear, dread, anger, or grief. Cognitively, we might experience racing or obsessive thinking, memory loss, or difficulty understanding. Somatically we might notice our heart racing, sweaty palms, or constriction of breath or muscle tension. Spiritually, we might question our beliefs or faith, or lose our sense of meaning. All of these symptoms are ones we tend to want to dis-own or avoid.

Whether neurotic anxiety, usually prefaced by calling forth the emotional, cognitive, somatic, or spiritual blocks that are being dis-owned; or by honoring and encouraging the experience of healthy anxiety during a moment of paradoxical insight, the Intuitives are often the deepest place where the therapist meets the client within their relationship. By the therapist allowing him/herself to be aware of and responsive to their own intuitive experience, we are offered the opportunity to have the visceral experience of existential anxiety with our client, and to provide them (and, of course, ourselves) the chance to move through this powerful learning, coming out the other side with a clearer understanding of paradox and the ability to choose for ourselves.

# Summary

The Intuitives are both tools by which we come to understand our lived experiences in the world, and a process by which we make meaning of these experiences. Although perhaps not limited to our senses, these are the primary modes by which we come to "know" others and ourselves, often when words themselves are not enough. In my experience, our kinesthetic, auditory, and visual senses are the most pronounced in their capacity to provide us with unspoken information. Kinesthetically, this information arises through body sensations, such as tight muscles, headaches, sleepiness, pain, and other physical sensations that do not seem to fit with our own life experience of our body. Or it perhaps might exaggerate symptoms we are familiar with in order to get the message across. Additionally, the kinesthetic intuitive also presents as emotions that we feel in the midst of the therapeutic relationship, often feelings that clients are dis-owning. Auditorally, we might "hear" words or phrases, or fragments of music that seem to insist on being attended to. Visually, we might "see" (sometimes this "seeing" is more a knowing of) images, often that appear to be metaphorical in nature, or colors, or scenes from a movie. Again, with any of these, there is a certain insistence on them being attended to. Once named within the therapeutic encounter, they lose their potency.

We each seem to have one of the Intuitives that is more finely tuned than the others, although any one of them might come forward in our work. They are most profoundly useful as they arise in the moment within a session, when the client and therapist make a connection that is vibrant and alive. This moment of contact is when the self-in-relational field brings the past and future into the present, and time seems to lose its linear edge. By naming what we are intuiting, we are able to throw the dis-owned energy back into this relational field. This gives the client an opportunity to explore its meaning. Although most often, because this is a highly connected moment for the client as well as the therapist, the client is able to re-own the energy, it is always important for the therapist to name it yet be willing to let it go simultaneously. It is less a moment of interpretation, and more an opportunity to explore a mystery. Whether it is "right" for the therapist is not the point. It is whether the client finds it useful in his or her own creation of her/himself that is important.

Finally, beyond the usefulness of these Intuitives for the therapist and the therapeutic work, it is also a tool that can be culled and honed within the client's experience of him or herself. If we can guide the client to a level of awareness of their own intuitive knowledge, and how to access and use it in their life, then we are helping our clients find that balance so necessary for living an authentic experience.

# V

# Contextual Existential Assessment

"Ultimately, man should not ask what the meaning of his life is, but rather he must recognize that it is he who is asked."—Victor Frankl

As discussed briefly in the first chapter, I have a firm belief that assessment is a crucial tool in our clinical work. Despite the fact that Existential counseling and psychology has professed an avoidance of anything that might be interpreted as "criteria" for clinical understanding, each writer and practitioner of Existential counseling and therapy certainly utilizes strategies to help them understand the lived experiences of their clients. From a Contextual Existential framework, then, I am laying the groundwork for certain areas of assessment in our work with others. Following the key components of Contextual Existentialism as outlined in Chapter 1, this chapter will focus on a number of core areas for assessment. With the belief that solid assessment offers us a doorway towards understanding, I will encourage you to take into consideration some specific concepts and questions.

Keep in mind that assessment is an on-going process, in and of itself paradoxical in nature. Thus, while considering these questions and concepts, it is equally important to hold them as a framework for theoretical understanding, not necessarily how the client will view or describe their experiences. Thus, as previously stated, we must use them for *our* benefit, and be willing to let these understandings go if they do not fit for the client. They are mechanisms by which we can make sense of someone else's experience, not to be interpreted as the experience itself. In addition, assessment is an on-going process, one that happens during each session/interaction with a client.

Although we might keep in mind previous understandings, within Contextual Existential theory it is imperative that we greet each new interaction as a mystery. This allows us to come to new understandings as each new story unfolds. Remember, we as human beings, are constantly "be-coming," thus the only "truth" that can be understood, is that which is shared in the moment. While past and present stories may sound and look similar, we must understand that there will always be nuances of difference, solely because the present moment already has incorporated and shifted what has already passed. Yet, with these assessment techniques, we are better able to respond to the client in ways that might move the therapeutic process forward.

There are several concepts that are important to remember and consider as we work with any client:

*Capacity for self-awareness:* We must firmly remember and believe that all humans have the capacity for self-awareness. As such, it demands that we hold a certain *faith* in the process and the ability for each client (and ourselves) to come to an understanding of their experience. Our job is not to answer or interpret for them, although often it is useful to share our experiences of being with them, which includes our feelings, thoughts, and images. Ultimately, however, the work is theirs to do, thus we must gently push them towards their center, towards their potentiality, and towards their ability to live authentically.

*Homeostasis:* Because the natural inclination in all humans is toward homeostasis, we must always remember that when clients present themselves to us, it is because some element of their being is out of balance. It is required of us to pay attention to which domain seems most over-utilized both in that moment with us, and in their day to day lives. Thus, attending to the somatic (physical), cognitive (psychological), emotional, and spiritual (meaning-making) domains in each client are always our intent.

*Contextual experience:* We are beings-in-relationship. We come to know ourselves through our contact with others and our world. Thus, in order to understand our clients, we must understand the social, familial, cultural, political, and environmental influences that shape their (and our) experiences, and thus our understandings of them (and ourselves). Within this it is useful to understand the Existential concepts of the *Umwelt* (the world around us/the biological world including our personal biology as well as the environment/ecological world within which we exist), the *Mitwelt* (the world with, our community of humans, our relationship with others both individually and communally. Here in particular is where we must understand the role of social and cultural influences. In addition, one might consider how we relate to our environment.), the *Eigenwelt* (our own world, our relationship with our "self" and how we come to understand "self." This is our intra-personal world), and the *Überwelt* (the world above/beyond us and the planet. This is our spiritual world, whether religious or secular. It is how we come to understand that which connects us to others and the planet, to the universe, and to any transcendent experience.) These four "worlds" are deeply inter-connected, even as they explain more specific segments of our experience and ways of relating.

*Paradoxes of living:* To "be" in the world, means to deal with the paradoxical experience of our self-knowledge and self-in-relation. Although it can be said that there are multiple obstacles to living in the world authentically, Existentialism, and thus Contextual Existentialism (which stresses additional aspects in italics) posits that there are four universal conditions that all human beings struggle with in our attempts to navigate our lives. These are (1) our awareness of our ultimate aloneness (isolation) even as we strive for connection with others *(and our world; here I would stress the need to attend to and understand how our environment/ecological world impacts our psyche)*; (2) finding/creating meaning in a world that often seems meaningless *(which incorporates the concept of faith)*; (3) our awareness of our mortality (death) and non-being *(metaphorical "death"—our fear of losing our sense of "self" or potentiality)* even as we strive to live our lives fully and in the moment; and (4) freedom (our ability and inescapable awareness of choice) even as we must accept responsibility for the consequences of these choices.

*Healthy and neurotic anxiety:* Healthy anxiety arises as the result of our awareness of one or more of the paradoxes. It is natural to experience anxiety as we confront these "givens of existence," as it is the energetic force which, if attended to, can motivate us to transcend our here-and-now "self" and create our future. We are constantly a self-in-motion (transcendence), creating and re-creating how we choose to be in the world. It is only when we become immobilized by this anxiety (stuck) that the energy becomes static (thus exaggerated and neurotic). In this "choosing not to choose" we move out of the moment and become fixated on the past or the future, unable to live authentically. Healthy anxiety can arise in the context of inter-personal anxiety, that which arises as a result of imbalance or denied relationships with others or the world, and intra-personal anxiety, that which arises when we are out of contact with aspects of our "self" and all of the potential we hold. Existential anxiety cuts underneath both of these to speak to the unbridgeable gap between ourselves and others that can never be solved. It is this Existential anxiety that can most motivate us towards our authenticity. Contextual Existentialism would add to this an understanding that both healthy and neurotic anxiety are connected to, and experienced within, the four "worlds," namely, the *Umwelt* (how we experience anxiety physiologically and in connection to our physical world), the *Mitwelt* (how we experience anxiety in response to lack of connection to others or the world), the *Eigenwelt* (how we experience anxiety in response to a lack of a sense of our own potentiality), and the *Überwelt* (how we experience anxiety in response to crises of meaning).

*Healthy and neurotic guilt:* Like anxiety, guilt too arises out of a response to internal and/or external experiences. Guilt also can serve a healthy purpose or become neurotic. From an Existential perspective, healthy guilt is that which is in response to an individual's choosing against his/her own value and moral structure as well as within those moments when we choose in ways that are contrary to our authenticity. Whenever we make choices at any level or within any of the paradoxes which moves us away from authentic "being" and homeostasis, we are subject to healthy guilt. If we listen to this "guilt against health" then we can choose in ways that moves us forward in our life process. Neurotic guilt, on the other hand, arises in response to our choosing based on externalized perceptions of our world and ourselves. When we have come to define ourselves based on what others want or expect from us, we are more likely to make choices that move us away from our authenticity. The same holds true when we make choices from a belief in a static "self," one defined by our history and/or biology alone. When we feel guilty because we are choosing based on external expectations, it is because we have lost our sense of our own potentiality and feel overly responsible for people and events that are outside of our control. Neurotic guilt keeps us stuck, and thus unable to choose and create our future. It often results in "choosing not to choose."

*Intuition and tacit knowing*: How do we learn to listen to ourselves, to tap into our potentiality in order to find the answers? Becoming a healthy individual requires us to navigate the world, sorting out what are our understandings, beliefs, and meanings. We are often confronted with what others expect us to be, which is not necessarily who we are. The pressures to conform to external guidelines can often leave us out of touch with our central "knowing" of who we are in the world. In a more mechanized and materially oriented world, it is easy to support some aspects of our being while denying or minimizing others. In U.S. culture, for example, there is a high value on intellect over feelings, leaving many of us out of touch with our emotions. This often also leads as well, to a lack of awareness of our somatic self. As such, we move out of homeostasis early in life. Learning to regain this balance requires us to listen more carefully to our inner knowledge, to trust and have faith that in fact, we do have the answers. Intuition, as previously described, is the bridge to this knowledge, and tacit knowing (knowledge without words) is often one kind of knowing that we more easily disavow because it is not cognitive in nature. When we can learn to attend to our inner knowledge through mechanisms such as meditation, focusing, and in-dwelling; we are more able to trust and use this tacit knowing to make healthy choices. It is through intuition (and what I have previously defined as the Intuitives) that this information comes to light.

*Metaphor as a language of meaning:* I have just spoken about the power of intuition and more specifically, tacit knowing. But how does our use of the Intuitives bring this tacit knowledge to the forefront? I would argue that this is the role of metaphor. Metaphor provides a language of making meaning of our inner knowledge that may not have "words" with which to describe it. Our soma (body) is one form with which this metaphor might present itself. Our body is giving us information every minute of our lives, often translating unheard messages in a fashion that grabs our attention. For example, when we are out of touch with our emotions, the energy that they create needs to be expressed somewhere. The body is an easy receptor. What we often call "stress" can actually be dis-placed emotions held in our body. We feel tight or tense. Our muscles hurt, we get stiff backs or necks; stomachaches or headaches. In short, the ignored energy goes somewhere. This is an example of soma as metaphor. One way or another, the message will be heard. At other times, we have strong feelings that seem to come from nowhere. These too are messages. Or perhaps, we have images (like in our dreams, but also while we are awake) that invoke some knowledge, even though it may not make sense. We are reminded of a story, or a movie, or a piece of music. All of these can be examples of the language of metaphor. Knowledge that needs to come through, that for whatever reason, we are unable to put into concrete words, or are unable or are not ready to verbalize directly. As clinicians, attending to these metaphors as they arise from our clients, or within ourselves as we work with our clients, can be extremely useful in moving the work forward. I will discuss the use of metaphor as a therapeutic tool in the later chapter on treatment, specifically as it relates to transference.

# Foreground and Background

The terms *foreground* and *background* have been used in psychological theory for some time. Within Contextual Existentialism, the terms foreground and background are being used to speak to what happens in the therapeutic encounter, more specifically, what the clinician needs to pay attention to in terms of information, experiences while with the client, and most importantly, the kinds of questions one should be considering. These questions focus on both the client and counselor/therapist experience. The clinician should be interested in how the client is evidencing his or her life through the lens of Contextual Existential theory, as well as assessing his/her own experience being with the client. When we speak of "background" in this sense, we are speaking to the client's experience, both historically from the story (or stories) they are telling , and in the present encounter with the counselor/therapist. When we speak of "foreground" here, we are speaking to the experience of the clinician, both in terms of his or her present encounter with the client, but also to their historical, and experiential understanding of themselves.

The following are questions to consider when assessing each client/clinician encounter. It should be stressed once again, that assessment is an on-going process, not one that only takes place during the first session. Even as we consider these assessment questions, we must be willing to let them go if they do not seem to fit for the current therapeutic experience, or if they move the work out of the here and now. While the information we might gather in each encounter can certainly be "stored away" for future reference, we must always remember that from encounter to encounter, what the client brings in can shift, change, and be presented in a myriad of ways. The following questions are meant to help clinicians come to understand the experience of their client's lives, and as such are internally driven. We are not asking the clients these questions, rather asking ourselves what we understand of our clients experience within a Contextual Existential frame.

## Background

Here we are considering information that helps us to understand how the client is "being" in the world. Understood through the lens of Contextual Existentialism, the purpose is to help the therapist in responding to the therapeutic encounter in a way that might move the process forward while staying fully present. There is no hierarchy to these questions, and in a here-and-now experience, these questions often open us to other areas of inquiry. Some of the answers to these questions become clearer over several encounters, revealing patterns of "being-in-the-world" that are longer term (thus often revealing areas of stuckness). Remember, these are questions being considered internally by the clinician, not questions being asked of the client.

1. Who is this client? What are the cultural/contextual influences that I need to be aware of? (Here the use of the ADDRESSING model can be of great help).

2. How "present" is the client? How well are they able to engage in the here and now, rather than the past or future?

3. As we listen to their story, what paradoxes might be at play here? What are the symptoms and how is anxiety being manifested?

4. What appears to be their primary relational style (compliant, detached, aggressive)?

5. What appears to be their primary domain of interaction with their world (which domain seems to be over-utilized at the expense of the others, thus leading to being out-of-balance)? Is it cognitive, somatic, emotional, or spiritual?

6. What appears to be their level of development (aesthetic, ethical, religio-spiritual)? Are they able to move fluidly between them, or do they appear stuck at or between levels?

7. How well are they relating to each of the four worlds (Umwelt, Mitwelt, Eigenwelt, Überwelt)? Is their anxiety manifesting more in one than the others?

## Foreground

Here we are considering assessment questions that will help us to understand and remember our experience being-with our client. What is our experience and what do we know about ourselves that might help us to stay present and attend to the client and the energy of the therapeutic relationship? Again, remember, these are internally asked questions, and ones that must constantly be re-assessed throughout the encounter, and from encounter to encounter. Sometimes, patterns will emerge in our experiences with our client that will help us to understand their experiences in the world as well.

1. How present am I? How well am I able to stay in the here and now with my client?

2. How do I help the client stay in the here and now?

3. What am I experiencing as I sit with the client? (This is a strong indicator of the power of self-as-instrument in the therapeutic process. More discussion of this will occur in the chapter on treatment.) What am I noticing about my experience somatically? Emotionally? Cognitively? Spiritually?

4. What is my primary intuitive sense (visual, auditory, kinesthetic, olfactory, gustatory)?

5. What do I see (experience) in the client? Somatically? Emotionally? Cognitively? Spiritually?

The following case study will be utilized to portray how, as a clinician, we would utilize these foreground and background questions to assess our client from a Contextual Existential frame. I will start by offering a generic description of the client, followed by how I would answer the assessment questions throughout the course of the clinical work.

# Bryan

Bryan was a client I saw for about eight months several years ago. He came initially because his mother brought him. More accurately, she told him that if he was to continue living in her home, he needed to "get some help" as she experienced him as "changing," "developing attitude, and becoming angry and defiant." Bryan was not thrilled at the prospect of counseling, but came anyway. Needless to say, the beginning of our work was a bit rocky, but I give credit to him for sticking with it.

## Background

*1. Who is this client? What are the cultural/contextual influences that I need to be aware of? (Here the use of the ADRESSING model can be of great help).*

Bryan is a 16-year-old (A) African-American (R/N) male (G) youth from a middle class (E) background. He was raised Baptist (S) which is a strong force in his extended family. He identifies as heterosexual (S) and has no disabilities (D). He claims no indigenous heritage "unless you mean my people came here from Africa" (I). Bryan clearly has had different experiences from my own. Although I am mixed race, I look white and was raised in a white, middle to upper-middle class family. While I can understand the forces of oppression due to my experiences of being gay, it is still not the same experience as Bryan might have as an African-American male. He is straight. He is from a different generation. His religious background is different. I will need to pay attention to my biases so as not to allow them to compromise our work. Simultaneously, I will need to be aware of, and to encourage Bryan to speak from his own cultural history and experience, so that I might better understand who he is from moment to moment in our work.

*2. How "present" is the client? How well are they able to engage in the here and now, rather than the past or future?*

My experience being with Bryan tells me that he has difficulty being in the present. His storytelling with me tends to be future oriented, in that he is constantly talking about how things will be different (how *he* will be different) when he is 16, when he lives on his own, when he has power, money, etc. Although he occasionally talks from a past perspective, this is not common. He rarely speaks from the present. I suspect that to be in the moment is too painful for Bryan. To experience "what is" means to experience "who he is not."

*3. As we listen to their story, what paradoxes might be at play here? What are the symptoms and how is anxiety being manifested?*

Existentialism, and certainly Contextual Existential theory, posits that all human beings struggle with the paradoxes of living in the world, and that we all have the capacity for self-awareness. This transcends culture; however, it is also understood within Contextual Existential theory that how it plays out will be dependent on social, cultural, ecological and developmental factors. As such, I understand that although Bryan is 16, he still faces these paradoxes, and will express them in ways that are appropriate for his developmental process. What appear to be out front for Bryan are the paradoxes of freedom and responsibility, closely followed by meaning and meaninglessness. His stories speak to his experiences of victimization and his struggle with the choices he makes in response to his experiences. Interwoven through these stories are questions and comments about who he is in the world and what he believes and values. His symptoms manifest in impotent anger, and times of depression. In addition, his behavior appears to often be "out of control," and his body language speaks volumes. As we progress in our work, I have no doubt that issues of isolation and connection, and death and life will emerge. Of special importance will be my ability to understand the role of racism and other factors of oppression. In addition, how has it been for Bryan to be raised in an urban environment? Does he have a connection at all to the natural world? How have political, social and familial influences affected him? What is it like to be an adolescent in today's world?

*4. What appears to be their primary relational style? (compliant, detached, aggressive)?*

Bryan appears to have a primarily aggressive style of relating. It is, after all, what prompted his mother to bring him in. In the one session I had with both Bryan and his mother, she reported this as a pattern "ever since he was little." As Bryan's story unfolded, I came to hear his experience of living in a household where he often felt isolated and ignored. His behaviors (and his feelings and somatic orientation) demanded attention. What is interesting is that within several sessions, I witnessed the part of Bryan that was quiet, reflective, and quite compliant as well. The question becomes, how do we help Bryan respond to his here-and-now experience with the relational style that will be the healthiest in response to what is occurring at that point in time?

*5. What appears to be their primary domain of interaction with their world (which domain seems to be over-utilized at the expense of the others, thus leading to being out-of-balance)? Is it cognitive, somatic, emotional, or spiritual?*

This is a bit more difficult to discern early on in our relationship. But as time progresses, it appears that Bryan over-utilized his emotional domain, although followed closely by his cognitive. It seems most difficult for Bryan to allow himself to be in his body, and he is loathe (at this point) to explore any sense of spirituality or meaning making, despite the fact that the meaning/meaninglessness paradox continues to crop up in our work.

*6. What appears to be their level of development (aesthetic, ethical, religio-spiritual)? Are they able to move fluidly between them, or do they appear stuck at or between levels?*

Bryan, at this point, appears to be stuck mostly in the aesthetic, responding to his world in a very narcissistic way, attending to his wants and needs at the expense of any sense of relationality. However, he is bordering on emerging into the ethical level, albeit in ways that still seem aesthetically oriented. He is beginning to respond (react) to dualistic ways of thinking, but mostly informed by his own narcissistic sense of what is right or wrong, as opposed to the influence of the external social/cultural context. Some of this is starting to be tied to the ethics of external groups that influence Bryan, which speaks to his emerging sense of himself in relationship, even if these relationships are not necessarily healthy for him.

*7. How well are they relating to each of the four worlds (Umwelt, Mitwelt, Eigenwelt, Überwelt)? Is their anxiety manifesting more in one than the others?*

Bryan seems clearly to be relating within the Umwelt and the Eigenwelt. His tendency towards being stuck in the aesthetic speaks to his pre-occupation with the Umwelt, the biological world. His actions and responses to his experience tend towards self gratification, physically, sexually, and emotionally. On another level, the eco-psychological level, his being raised in an urban environment has left him out of touch with the ecological world. He has no sense of "place" and how his environment impacts him psychologically. Combined, these responses to the Umwelt feed his tendency towards attention to his Eigenwelt, the intra-personal domain. His symptoms speak volumes about his internal struggle with himself, thus leaving little time to explore his relationship with the Mitwelt (the relational world) or the Überwelt (the world above and beyond, the spiritual world).

## Foreground

*1. How present am I? How well am I able to stay in the here and now with my client?*

As it is with all of us, it takes practice (for myself in the process of meditation) to be able to stay more present in the here and now. With Bryan, it is not too much of a problem for me, although I cannot say that for my work with some other clients. Because my own tendency historically has been to revert to "past tripping," Bryan's focus on the future is not as much of a hook for me. However, in this work, it is always important to pay attention to our state of being-ness while with our client's. It is easy to be "coerced" into their avoidance of the moment if we don't pay attention to ourselves in the relationship.

*2. How do I help the client stay in the here and now?*

Because Bryan tends towards over reliance on his emotional and cognitive domains, it is useful for our work to encourage him to attend more to his somatic experience, especially early in our work. By stopping Bryan when he jumps into the future, and asking him to breathe and pay attention to what he is experiencing in his body (despite his resistance, and then we look at his experience of resistance), he is more able to come back into the present. As a result, his tendency towards emotional outbursts or over intellectualizing or rationalizing his experience is lessened. He is quite clear that he does not like to "go there," but he admits (over time) that the more he can stay present and centered, the more he is in contact with his anxiety and, eventually, his liberation. This takes time, but in some ways, because he is still an adolescent and not nearly as entrenched as older clients, he is able to free himself up sooner than I have experienced with other adult clients. In addition, by naming what my experience is being with Bryan, and what I notice being in the room with him, Bryan is more able to begin to notice his own experience in the here and now of its unfolding. His awareness of himself grows.

*3.    What am I experiencing as I sit with the client? What am I noticing about my experience somatically? Emotionally? Cognitively? Spiritually?*

As I am primarily kinesthetically oriented, and because Bryan is most disconnected from his soma, I often feel strong physiological and emotional responses when I am working with Bryan. The more resistant he is to being in his body, the more I notice physical symptoms. The more his body responds to what is going on in the room together, the more I notice strong emotions in myself. As I work with him to come back into the here and now, the symptoms I experience usually increase. I might notice feeling tight or tense in my neck and arms, or conversely, as he avoids feeling what is underneath his anger and frustration, I often experience the sadness, pain, and/or grief that he often is suppressing. As I name this experience of being with him, he is more able over time to recognize these same symptoms in his own field of experience. Simultaneously, my experience of these symptoms dissipates. In addition, because I am so kinesthetically attuned, I am also aware of the role of the Umwelt, particularly the ecological/environmental aspects of this world. I can sense the dis-connect that Bryan experiences in his relationship with his external environment. Since this lack of awareness spans the Umwelt, and paradoxically also the Mitwelt (how he relates to the external environment of which he is also a part), it becomes crucial that I pay attention to anything he might bring to our work that speaks to this dis-connect. Casual language referring to a lack of connection to nature or perhaps to the urban experience of violence can be indicators of dis-ease within these domains.

*4.    What is my primary intuitive sense (visual, auditory, kinesthetic, olfactory, gustatory)?*

As stated above, my primary intuitive is kinesthetic, as evidenced by the physical and emotional sensations I experience with Bryan. My secondary intuitive tends to be visual. I often "see" images, colors, or visual metaphors that when shared with Bryan, most often resonate with him, and help him to name or understand some aspect of his in-the-world experience.

*5.    What do I see (experience) in the client? Somatically? Emotionally? Cognitively? Spiritually?*

Although Bryan can easily share certain emotions (anger and frustration most noticeably), he is cut off from many other emotions. In fact, his over compensation with expressing anger and frustration actually takes him away from (as a defensive measure) his fear, pain, and grief. With Bryan specifically, his body language tends to be quite tense, especially evident in his neck, shoulders, and arms. When I am with him, his shoulders often tighten and come forward, and his hands are clenched into fists. He is most often not aware of this, which speaks to how dis-connected he is to his body. In addition, Bryan has over utilized his cognition in order to intellectualize and rationalize his experience. By naming this as it happens in our work, and encouraging him to pay more attention to what he knows somatically and emotionally, he is able to begin the process of questioning his assumptions and thought processes. Ultimately, as we work to integrate and bring more balance to his use of his domains, our work takes us slowly towards issues of meaning making. While Bryan has decried his formal Baptist up-bringing, he is just beginning to speak of what he finds meaningful and important in his life. As his own development progresses, especially as he moves from the aesthetic stance to the ethical, he hopefully will begin to be more in contact with the Mitwelt, and eventually the Überwelt.

## Summary

From a Contextual Existential perspective, it is important to see assessment as a useful part of the therapeutic process. Rather than it being a limited and often "frozen in time" perspective about our client, one which then can lead to generalizations, covert biases, and treatment based on history only, assessment from this perspective allows us to utilize information that plays itself out in the moment, and thus avoids becoming dogmatic or a label that paints a picture of the client that never changes. It is by seeing assessment as a process by which we come to some understanding of our client's experience as it moves and changes from moment to moment, rather than a product by which we make all future decisions, that allows us to stay present and fully engage in the client-therapist relationship. Although relevant patterns may emerge, indicative of longer-term areas of "stuckness" for our client, assessment serves primarily as a tool that can be used and discarded as new information unfolds. And new information will always reveal itself, as each of us, as human beings, is constantly in a state of transition, even as paradoxically we experience aspects of ourselves as static.

It is hoped that as clinicians (and clients) and more importantly, human beings; attending to these concepts and assessment questions we can more fully develop our "self-as-instrument," the most important and beneficial tool at our disposal in this therapeutic art.

# VI

# Diagnosis, the DSM, and Language

"Madness need not be all breakdown. It may also be break-through. It is potential liberation and renewal as well as enslavement and existential death."
—R. D. Laing

As discussed briefly in Chapter 1, Existential Psychology on the whole has attempted to avoid categorization of any sort. Not only has there been a strong desire to resist becoming technique driven, but also a resistance to utilizing any sort of formal assessment or diagnostic approach to therapeutic work. The premise for this is understandable. Since Existentialism as a whole supports the arena of subjectivity over objectivity (even as it attempts to dig deeper to that place of paradox), any move to adhere to a set pattern that would generalize behavior or experience is counter to the core beliefs of the theory. In addition, it potentially might create a possible "standardization" of theory that would leave individual practitioners little room for personal interpretations. Yet, as I stated earlier, I am not sure this suspicion is truly called for. I would argue instead that we could hold room for personal interpretation of the core Existential concepts *and* have room for the utilization of assessment tools and diagnostic information. Is this not a paradoxical stance? As long as we remember to utilize such tools for therapeutic understanding, not as determinant labels, we can avoid the risk that so many of the other psychological theories have fallen prey to. That is, the risk of taking the human being out of the process, and reducing them (and us) to sets of drives, biological triggers, cognitive and behavioral patterns, and yes, even spiritual forces. In addition, even with the importance of understanding cultural context, we have to be careful not to use this as a means of defining *who we are*, but rather as a frame for understanding *how we have come to be*.

Beyond this, I would argue that as practitioners who work with other practitioners from a variety of theoretical beliefs, it is imperative that we have a common language with which to understand each other and our work. It is foolish to believe that we will only ever work with those others who think like ourselves.

Perhaps it is even dangerous, as it would never offer us an opportunity to debate our ideas in an environment of difference. I believe that it is by such debates and discussions, that we can become clearer in our thinking and beliefs. The challenge of speaking from this place forces us away from complacency and stagnation, and towards a deepening and widening of our knowledge. As such, an understanding and working knowledge of tools such as the DSM are crucial to our participation in the larger context of our field. Seeing it as a language that is shared by the psychological and counseling communities and not a set of labels describing a conformative view of human behavior allows us to utilize it to support, rather than detract from our Existential work.

Remember, the DSM (Diagnostic and Statistical Manual of Mental Disorders) was created not as a manual for the betterment of the insurance industry, or the managed care industry, which have co-opted it for their own use, but for the mental health community as a way to broaden our understanding of the many facets of human behavior. It is a constantly evolving manual, with more recent attention being given to the role of gender and culture in how we understand behavior. Yes, it is more often than not misused within and outside of our field. Yes, it is often taught in such a way that it does wind up de-humanizing us. And yes, it has a long way to go to truly encompass the divergent patterns that emerge as a result of cultural differences. However, remember that it is people who label, not the DSM. By our participation in the discussion of human suffering, perhaps we might have an impact on how the larger counseling and psychological community can remember that it is people we are treating, not diagnoses.

# What is Diagnosis?

*To distinguish from, to know* (m-w.com, 2007). This is the formal definition of diagnosis. Coming from its Greek roots, and later New Latin translation, the focus of diagnosis is to come to know something about a phenomenon. In the case of counseling and psychology, diagnosis is the opportunity to "come to know" the phenomenon of human behavior. In purely medical terms, diagnosis is usually related to examining and understanding symptoms that make up a medical disorder. This unfortunately has also become the hallmark in psychology (and to some degree counseling), particularly as it attempts to make the field into a quasi-medical one. Most humanistically oriented counselors and therapists question whether or not the field itself is not more an art than a science. I would have to agree. Unless we can re-define science to incorporate the realm of qualitative description and understanding, then perhaps calling it an art is the most accurate description. Yet, let us understand that in the arena of art, there can be very clear "understandings" of the nature of different phenomenon.

Thus, I would argue, that from a humanistic place, diagnosis is a useful tool in our growing understanding of any individual's experience. For a clinician to attempt to know and understand another human being's experience is the first step in one's ability to help. I can hear your story, but unless I can translate that story into a frame of reference with which I have come to understand the human psychological condition, I am useless. I strongly believe that being a "listener" offers a very useful function. To be heard unconditionally is imperative in the process of coming to know oneself. However, when one is experiencing a disrupted life, then listening is often not enough. Certainly, when clients come to see a professional clinician, they are hoping for more than just a listener. This is where diagnosis comes in. Diagnosis, at least from a Contextual Existential perspective, becomes the bridge between the client's story, and the clinician's understanding of that story. Diagnosis, in this phenomenological way is the tool that translates the experience, through the frame of theory, into an articulated form that gives shape to the underlying etiology of the experience itself. It is an ontological approach to assessment and diagnosis. Through this phenomenological lens, we *come to know* (to diagnose) an individual's experience of being. It is from this diagnostic impression that the clinician is able to have some understanding of what is going on, thus a place from which to offer guidance.

The trick, from this theoretical bias, is to form this impression such that it offers a useful platform from which to respond, yet simultaneously, being willing to let this formulation go if it doe not fit for the client him or herself. This, of course, does not mean that the diagnostic information is useless (or even wrong), but it is important to always follow our clients, for it is their story, their process, that is at the center of this dialogue. Keeping the work in the here and now requires us to follow their lead, not our own agenda, particularly if the agenda becomes one of proving ourselves right. Of course, assessment (or asking the right questions, gathering the information—both verbal and non-verbal) that can help us to come to a diagnosis is equally important. The previous chapter focused more fully on the assessment process within a Contextual Existential approach. In this chapter I want to come back to the question and nature of diagnosis within this theoretical framework, especially as it relates to our work with client's, and equally as important, our ability to work with other clinicians.

## A Process, Not an Outcome

So now, we have come to some understanding of what a diagnosis is, and (hopefully) why it might be useful. How else do we distinguish diagnosis within a Contextual Existential frame, differently from more traditional therapeutic practice? First and foremost, diagnosis here is not a noun, but rather more an adjective. It is a qualifying description of a moment in time (or, in many cases, a series of moments in time, existentially speaking. Not from past to present to future, but rather a reflection of how past, present and future are all captured simultaneously in experience). It is not the answer, nor is it the label of any individual's totality of being. Here, it is meant to capture a sense of Contextual Existential experience; whether it is the Existential paradox, the level of moral/value development, or the relational style within which an individual might be struggling. It might also be a way of capturing the worldview with which the person is currently being held, the Mitwelt, Eigenwelt, Umwelt, or Überwelt. In all cases, it certainly is a way to understand the healthy or neurotic anxiety that is being evidenced. It is not a describer of *who* our clients are, but rather *how and what* they are experiencing that is causing dis-ease (one's disconnection from one's potentiality). Finally, it is a way to understand their pathology. Here, I am using this word (again, often mis-used by many in more "scientifically" oriented fields) from its Greek root "pathos" which translates as "suffering." How is this client suffering? What is at the core of the suffering? How do I need to understand (to come to know—to diagnose) this suffering, in order to help?

# A Shared Language

If we have come to understand the nature of our client's suffering from a Contextual Existential perspective, how then, do we communicate this in a way that is more universally understood in the professional field of counseling and psychology? Again remember, that despite the fact that the DSM has been historically co-opted by the medical community (more specifically psychiatry) and the insurance companies in order to make the criteria of diagnosis an easily measurable one (focusing primarily on behavior); the original intent of the manual was to insure a common language that could be used across theoretical lines. Despite the fact that the research that went into classifying disorders is highly culturally biased (you may read this as *white, heterosexual, middle- to upper-class male*); there have been some strong movements within the past revisions to encourage alternative voices to be heard, as well as to broaden the understanding of cultural factors that impact assessment, diagnosis, and treatment. In addition, more recent discourses about the evolution of the DSM (we are currently using the DSM-IV-TR) have shown us how, despite the verbiage about scientific evidence, that the bulk of the manual and particularly the classification of disorders is really a reflection of a highly subjective and anecdotal process by which contributors discuss their own clinical experience with specific problem areas and diagnoses (APA, 2000).

There is still a long way to go with this; however I choose to be optimistic. I say this primarily because I do not believe that these diverse voices are willing any longer to stay silent. In addition, as larger disciplines, counseling and psychology have begun to see the relevant nature of exploring not only biology in relation to human psychological dysfunction, but also to take more seriously the role of social, cultural and environmental factors. Everything old is new again! So, it is with some hope, that we can expect, over time, the voices that speak to both somatic and spiritual elements of human behavior to be heard. Again! This more holistic way of thinking, which has been with many cultures over thousands of years, is beginning to be paid attention to. Witness the surging interest in alternative medicine! I must admit, I laugh at times as I hear that word "alternative," when in fact much of the basis for this approach has been around far longer than allopathic medicine. However, having said that, I believe it is important within the larger health movement to see this as a sign of our development.

I have diverged a bit here, so let me steer us back to the role of the DSM in all of this, especially as it relates to our function as existentially oriented practitioners. Just as the role of culture has begun to have an impact on how we approach psychological understanding, so too I believe, we as phenomenologists can also offer insights into the nature of human suffering. However, we can only do so if we take a seat at the table, rather than dismiss the rest of the field as if they had little to offer us, or as the enemy. It does us (and our clients) no good if we, to coin a proverbial phrase, "throw the baby out with the bath water." To be taken seriously within our profession, it is important that each of us study and learn the diagnostic categories of the DSM so that we can have educated discussions with our peers as we explore our varied understanding of what is at the root of these "dis-orders" (being "out of order" is not such a bad definition of the experience of suffering that our client's bring to us, although we might equally think of it as being out of balance, or movement away from authenticity). More so, by translating these diagnoses into Contextual Existential language, we not only formulate ways of thinking about our work, but we can also participate more effectively in consultations with our colleagues. Ultimately, we can also, hopefully, offer new suggestions for how to think about assessment, criteria, and classifications of disorders as new versions of the DSM unfold.

Irvin Yalom, in his book *Existential Psychotherapy* (1980), does a wonderful job of describing Existential understandings and interpretations of some common diagnostic areas. Beyond the natural discussion of anxiety and the related disorders, there are some nice descriptions of an Existential view of symptoms of depression, psychosis, addictive behaviors, trauma, stress, sexual symptoms, somatic symptoms, eating related symptoms, and dissociation. In addition, his work discusses the role that Existential theory and practice can play in not only individual counseling and therapy, but also in group and relationship work.

# Back to Bryan

In our last chapter, we were introduced to Bryan, a 16-year-old African-American male brought to counseling with me by his mother. In assessing Bryan from a Contextual Existential perspective, we came to see the paradoxes at play, his dominant relational style, where he was in his meaning making development, and how he interacted with his world. If we look at Bryan from a traditional diagnostic perspective, taking into consideration his history, his mother's report, and his noticeable behaviors, we might come to the conclusion that we are dealing with an adolescent with a conduct disorder. In knowing more about his history of who he hangs out with, and how his behavior is often different when alone versus with (some of) his friends, we might go further as to state this conduct disorder is of the group type. He has gotten in trouble with certain friends for physical intimidation, petty theft, and general trouble making, both in school and beyond. In fact, this is the diagnosis that Bryan came in with from his previous therapeutic experience. He had been required to involve himself in counseling as a result of some altercations that occurred on school grounds the year before. While his previous clinician seemed to understand that there were circumstances to be explored that might help in understanding Bryan's behavior, *who Bryan is* appeared to be overlooked at the expense of both where he came from and what he did. Somewhere along the line, Bryan's story was never listened to, his experience never attended to. With the rush to "fix" the problem behaviors, Bryan got lost.

On one hand, his diagnosis of Conduct Disorder, Group Type is fitting. His behaviors meet the criteria as outlined in the DSM-IV-TR (APA, 2000). As part of a larger inter-disciplinary team, it would be important for me to know this, and to know what it means. I could engage in dialogue with colleagues from a variety of different practical and theoretical backgrounds, and we would all be sharing a common language. I would understand that from a variety of different theoretical perspectives, Bryan might be viewed as being conduct disordered (i.e., his behavior might define who he is). From other perspectives, Bryan's behavior might be seen as adaptive to his early childhood experiences. From still others, Bryan's diagnosis might reflect an understanding of the biological forces causing a disease. From my own understanding, the behaviors would merely reflect Bryan's attempt to mediate living an authentic life in a world that does not necessarily offer an environment where this is easy. I would understand that Bryan's state of being-ness is not static, but rather fluid and able to grow and change from moment to moment. I would also understand that for reasons unknown to me, Bryan has become stuck in his natural anxiety (thus it has become neurotic), and his behaviors are evidence of this.

My work then, is to try to understand Bryan's experience of being-in-the-world, to listen to his story as it unfolds from moment to moment, and to have faith in his inherent capacity to know himself fully, and thus to be able to transcend himself and live his life authentically. Part of this process will be to help him come to his own self-awareness; how his history and his future are part of his present experience. He will need to be in contact with all of his domains, physical/somatic, cognitive, emotional, and spiritual. This allows us to take into consideration any of the factors that might be influencing Bryan's "symptoms," including early experience, current environmental factors, and yes, even any physiological factors that have an impact on his behavior and his life. He will need to come to understand how he relates to not only himself but to his world and others in it.   I will need to remember that his diagnosis and the criteria that describe it, only describes Bryan's actions in specific moments of his life, not all of who he is. While useful for conveying a theme in his life, it is not a description of him. Only Bryan, with support in his process of becoming more mindful, can decide who Bryan will become.

# Conclusion

In summation, I encourage all of you who may be reading this to strongly consider attending to two things. First it is imperative that you learn and keep up with the changes going on around the use of the DSM as a diagnostic tool. With this, remember that the DSM itself does not "label," rather it is clinicians who do so. Pay attention to your use of language. Do not fall into the trap of dehumanizing our clients. They are not "schizophrenics" or "borderlines" or "manic-depressives." For that matter, they are not "neurotics" either. They are people *with* symptoms of suffering. They are human beings experiencing "psychosis" or "depression" or "neurosis." But first, they are human beings.

Secondly, in understanding the language of the DSM, (and again, I stress that what we are really doing is learning a foreign language), we can communicate effectively with our colleagues from the same "country," that of psychology/counseling/family therapy/social work. By having this ability to communicate effectively, we are able to broaden our understanding of the symptomology that is presenting itself, whether within our own clinical work, or within consultation with our peers. It is this shared capacity for understanding that will allow us to offer our perspectives in a way that they can be heard. Finally, remember, that even though we might utilize this DSM language to make connections to the larger professional community, it by no means defines how we do our work. We can, and should, still attend to using assessment and diagnosis within a Contextual Existential frame, connecting our understanding of causality in order to frame the context of our therapeutic work. Ultimately, and most importantly, recognize that this helps *us* to help our clients *and* that we need to paradoxically both hold this understanding and let it go simultaneously so that we may remain open and present moment to moment in our work. For it is here where the healing really happens, when our authentic and present potentiality meets our client's. Diagnosis informs our work, and us; it does not define it.

# VII

# Treating the Whole Person

"To dare is to lose one's footing momentarily. Not to dare is to lose oneself."
—Soren Kierkegaard

As with many intra-psychically oriented therapies, the focus of work with individuals within a Contextual Existential frame is to explore the inner world of the client. By understanding the client's worldview, in particular their individual experience of their world, we can better facilitate healing. Once this understanding is established, it is easier to then attend to the domain of the interpersonal world. In this chapter we will explore both the structure and content of the therapeutic interaction. Starting with the establishment of the therapeutic relationship, we will then focus on how one works within the "here and now," and the impact of this approach on both the client and the clinician. By understanding the role of "clinician as tool" we will see how a variety of interventions might be utilized with an individual client, inclusive of the role of transference and naming. More importantly, the necessity of including the whole person (both counselor/therapist and client) in the movement towards homeostasis and authenticity will be examined. A case study will be used to bring to light how this process works with a client.

## The Case of Lonny

As previously stated in Chapter 5, it is important to always consider the contextual life of the client. As such, a cultural assessment is necessary to our understanding of our client. Using a model, such as the Hays ADDRESSING model (2001) we can have a clearer understanding of the contextual experience of our client. Lonny is a 45-year-old (A) gay (S), white (of German and Irish descent) (E), male (G) American (U.S.) (N). His family of origin has lived in the

United States for several generations, mostly in Colorado and Utah. Lonny was raised Mormon (R), but was ex-communicated from the church due to his homosexuality. He reports no formal religious practice, but speaks of his own spirituality often. He describes this as an informal connection he feels with his "higher power." Lonny reports no disabilities (D, D), either physical or developmental. His family of origin was middle class (S), as is Lonny. He has no reported indigenous background (I). He works as an electrician doing independent contracting. He currently lives in the city. Lonny initially called because he had been experiencing suicidal thoughts and some obsessive thinking. A colleague of mine and a friend of his referred him to me.

## Establishing the Therapeutic Container

Remembering that healing happens within the relationship between counselor/therapist and client, it is crucial to first and foremost establish a container that allows the relationship to unfold in an environment that is safe. We must understand that clients come to us due to some level of imbalance in their lives. For whatever reason, they are struggling to live their lives authentically, and on some level are aware of this. It is what brings them through our door. If we believe in the core Contextual Existential concepts, then we understand that the movement towards homeostasis and authenticity is the natural "drive" towards living out our potentiality. Thus, clients present themselves in ways that evidence how they are stuck in this process. When stuck, healthy existential anxiety has become neurotic, and the symptoms demonstrate ways in which the individual compensates in order to avoid their true underlying experiences, in essence their own inner knowing of the choices they must make in order to move towards their center once again.

With this in mind, the structure of the therapeutic relationship is as important as the interventions one might use to guide clients toward themselves. In fact, it should be noted that to ignore structure inevitably leads to failed therapy. No matter how skilled one might be in the use of interventions, clients who do not experience a safe and nurturing environment will not engage in the unfolding story of their experience. They might "tell" a story, but it will not be connected to their lived experience. In short, the story will be told in a limited and "out of time" context. By establishing safety and trust, clients can come to trust their capacity to hold their own anxiety, and to live in the moment of their story. The clinician's ability to nurture this process, and attend to their own ability to stay in the here and now, allows the client to experience someone truly witnessing their lives. The ability of the counselor/therapist to be fully present and to model living their life authentically while with their client is powerful. In the face of this experience of authentic relationship, the client begins to trust in their own capacity for creating and re-creating themselves, for tapping into their own potentiality.

After a brief phone conversation to establish contact and explore availability for both Lonny and myself, we set our first appointment. I am always clear to potential clients that the first session is evaluatory for both of us. I come from a firm belief that not every client and clinician will be a good match. It is important that both parties come into this work feeling like a connection has been made, and that there is potential for the relationship to develop. Thus, the first session is really an opportunity to spend time together, to gain a sense of what brings the client to counseling/therapy at this specific time in their life, and to begin to form a relationship. As such, the evaluatory session is both similar to and different than any other sessions that may follow. Although the focus is to be in the here and now, there is still a need for the clinician to ask questions that will form an outline of how this client experiences their life. This is the ground from which all assessment will occur, and forms an image of the client from which the clinician will work. As stated previously in Chapter 5, assessment is a tool that helps the counselor/therapist to work with the client. However, even as we form some understanding of the client and what existential issues are at work, we must simultaneously be willing to "let go" of our perceptions so that we can attend to the story as it is being told in this current moment. This may also mean, "letting go" when our perceptions do not match the client's experience of their life.

Lonny comes to his first session on time, directly from his job. We undergo the formalities of the profession, which includes going over the paperwork mandated by the state and the profession. Although not exactly in line with how an Existential counselor/therapist might want to work, I see it as an opportunity to explain more succinctly how I work as a Contextual Existential clinician. This includes asking Lonny to sign my disclosure statement which explains my theoretical beliefs, our financial agreement form, and a form that explains why I do not keep case notes except under certain emergent or legal circumstances. Again, this gives me an opportunity to explore how my theoretical bias operates in practice, and why client notes are generally not useful. He can make an informed decision as to whether he is comfortable with this, or if he wants me to keep session by session documentation of our work. He asks questions that help him clarify the work we would undertake, signs all forms, and we move on.

At this point, I ask him to talk a bit about what triggered his picking up the phone and calling me. As he explains, I attend to his story and to him, listening and watching for any non-verbal information that also tells his story. In this session alone, do I step in more intentionally and guide the *content* of the story? I want to have some understanding of what has brought Lonny to this point, and what he hopes for and wishes. From an Existential perspective, client's wishes and wants are useful in how we come to understand their world experience. It is in this session that I also learn more about Lonny's cultural context, so that I have some ability to frame his experience within the culture of his world. It is important for me to always remember that his cultural background informs his worldview in some way. It is my job to consider this as we work together so that I do not presume to understand his life from my own cultural biases. At times, I will bring this cultural context to the forefront and ask questions that will elicit Lonny's understanding of how culture plays a role in his experience. In future sessions, I will want the work to unfold from whatever Lonny's experience is in the moment of our contact, rather than from my agenda. However, I will still work with some intentionality. Specifically, I will guide the sessions and Lonny by helping us both stay fully present and attending to all of what emerges in each encounter together.

Ultimately, as we continue to work together, I will attempt to offer a container for our work that is safe and authentic. I will hold our work together as sacred, and will listen and attend to Lonny's unfolding story with Rogers' (1989) unconditional regard. This does not mean that I will not have my own reactions or judgments, however, it is up to me to be clear about when these responses are about me, versus when they are in direct relationship to the work I am doing with Lonny. In the former, it is prudent to bracket these responses, and deal with them in my own therapeutic work or consultation. In the latter, they may prove to be useful responses that can be brought fully into the work with Lonny, as I will discuss later in this chapter.

## Foreground and Background

As discussed in the chapter on assessment, the concepts of foreground and background speaks to the assessment information that you, as clinician, stay aware of as you work with your client. This includes the information that speaks to your own experience in your life as well as when sitting with your client (the foreground), as well as the questions you are quietly asking yourself to discern what is going on for your client in their life (the background). The latter includes what paradox(es) might be in the forefront, the predominant relational style, and primary domain utilized. You are simultaneously using these understandings to guide your work with your client, even as you are following the client's here-and-now story and discarding these assessments, as they no longer are relevant or current for the client. This is a delicate balance, recognizing the historical coping mechanisms that have been employed even as you open the door for healing and change, to ways of being in the world that are more balanced and healthy. In addition, the background includes our understanding of the client's level of values development, and their ability (or not) to stay in the present.

Given this, as I work with Lonny over several sessions, I am able to glean the predominant "themes" that seem to speak to my Contextual Existential understanding of his lived experiences. With this in mind, I sense that Lonny's anxiety arises mostly within the isolation/connection paradox, with his predominant issues arising in relationships to himself and others. In this way, it appears that Lonny's anxiety arises most often in relation to his "Mitwelt" (his relational world), and his "Eigenwelt" (his "self" world, the world of his potentiality). Since Lonny is stuck in this anxiety, it has become neurotic. That is to say, he is frozen in it, rather than utilizing it to propel himself into his future. As we move through our work together over time, the remaining paradoxes emerge in what seem to be waves. As we touch on how Lonny plays out his relationships in the world, issues of meaning, freedom, and death/life present themselves. In addition, Lonny appears to have adopted the "compliant" relational style; being whoever he senses others want him to be, in order to not be alone. Lonny mostly lives in his mind, his cognitive domain. It seems that to survive in his life, it is safer to intellectualize and rationalize his life, rather than allow himself to feel his feelings (especially those that are most uncomfortable), be in his body, or connect to his spiritual/meaning-making capacity.

Lonny appears to have a difficult time staying in the present. His life seems to be spent mostly living in the past, that is to say, his actions, feelings, and thoughts seem to be in response to his life as it *was* experienced, rather than as it *is* experienced. Lonny's values development has been somewhat thwarted by this combination of past focus, his relational style, and his neurotic anxiety. As such, he appears stuck between the aesthetic and ethical levels of existence. While, over time, his reliance on these more "fixed" ways of being in the world begin to diminish, they have been useful coping mechanisms that have allowed him to survive in a world that he had experienced as historically unsafe. To some degree or other, he had projected these past coping mechanisms onto his current experiences as well. Following are examples of how these coping styles evidenced themselves in our work.

## Isolation & Desire for Connection and Compliant Relational Style

As Lonny tells his story in each session, it becomes clear that a theme surrounding the paradox of isolation and connection emerges. A focus of much of his storytelling is on his relationship with his current partner of 12 years, and of his relationship with his mother (primarily) and his father (secondarily). He moves back and forth between these stories, usually triggered by interactions that have occurred over the past week or so. In all of these relationships, Lonny shares example after example of how he is not getting his needs met, but simultaneously, continues to avoid sharing this with either his partner or his mother. Instead, he talks of how he attempts to find ways to figure out what they are wanting from him, in some hope that they might then reciprocate. He appears unaware that this is a subversive style of communicating, although he is becoming more aware that he is unhappy and frustrated.

Often in the story telling, there are opportunities to ask Lonny about his present state awareness, and more specifically, whether or not these feelings, body sensations, or experiences are familiar. Although this is difficult for Lonny, who often attempts to avoid the present in favor of the more comfortable past, he is able, with support, to speak from this present space. This, of course, often results in strong emotional and/or somatic responses (see below). Either way, this brings Lonny's history into the room with us; stories of his experiences of covert psychological and emotional incest by his mother. These historical experiences can be clearly connected to how Lonny chooses to relate in other relationships over his lifetime. Remember that we have come to understand that one of the conditions of living is our innate desire to connect even as we are aware at the deepest level, of our ultimate aloneness. Here we can clearly see how Lonny's natural desire to connect with others has been thwarted by an unhealthy and overly enmeshed relationship with his mother. His response to his isolation under these circumstances is to become compliant. This "compulsive compliance" was experienced early on in his development as his only defense within this unhealthy relationship, and the only way in which he could experience connection without being annihilated. With an abusive mother and a virtually invisible father (chances are, exhibiting a "detached" style), his natural drive towards balance was, by necessity, submerged in order to survive. This relational style worked. It both afforded him the ability to have some sense of connection, while concurrently suppressing his healthy anxiety resulting from the isolation/connection paradox. Without a healthy environment within which to develop, his ability to experience this healthy anxiety was stunted.

Unfortunately, over time he "forgot" that his healthy center existed, and thus began to live his life primarily from this defensive stance. He entered every relationship, including the relationship with himself, from this compliant stance. He came to believe that who he was, was contingent upon what others wanted him to be. However, that deepest part of himself was always there, and as he became an adult, began to more energetically offer him opportunities to experience his anxiety, thus opportunities to live more authentically. This is what brought Lonny into counseling/therapy, and what, over time, allows him to begin making different choices for his life. What we can see in this particular example is how the other paradoxes also are present, even if in the background. Here, the paradoxes of freedom (choice) and responsibility, as well as death and striving for life emerge as players in his struggle with isolation and connection.

In addition, the intimate relationship between the isolation and connection paradox, and the relational styles themselves are highlighted. What is, perhaps, the most important part of our work, is to understand that Lonny will play out this compliant style with me. In our work, he is often trying to be the client he thinks I want him to be, in order to get his need for connection met. My job is to point this out as it is happening in the moment, in order for Lonny to have a real time, visceral experience of his anxiety as it emerges. Then, we move towards understanding what other choices he has in his relationship with me. This includes making his wishes and wants known to me, thus experiencing the difference of having a relationship where someone honors his voice and experience rather than sublimate it for their own needs. Of course, this does not mean that just by voicing one's wishes, that one will always get what one wants, but then too, we have opportunities to see the range of choices we have. Then we can make a decision that will enhance rather than detract from our authenticity. In our work together, there will be times that Lonny will not get what he wants from me, and, most importantly, he will experience me as someone who allows him to have his feelings and responses to this without abandoning (or annihilating) him.

*Living in His Head and in His Past*

As stated earlier, Lonny tends towards living in the past rather than the present. This is strongly connected to his choice to over utilize his intellect at the expense of his body, emotions, and spirit. By living in his head, Lonny is able to easily avoid the experience of his healthy anxiety as it arises, thus responding to the world from his historical experience, and with the defenses that had served him so well growing up. The problem currently is that these defenses are no longer working, and his natural drive towards homeostasis and authenticity are calling him to his potentiality, which requires choosing to live in the present. One very obvious way that living in the past shows up in our sessions is in the language that Lonny uses. When asked to speak to his current experience, he most often (in our early work) responded with statements about his past.

> "Lonny, tell me about how you are feeling right now?" "I don't know. Yesterday, Drew came home really angry, so we didn't have a chance to talk about whether or not we'll sell the house." or "Lonny, I'm noticing that as you are telling me about your conversation with you mother, you're fists are clenching. What are you feeling?" "I'm thinking about how my mom always does this to me, turns everything I say around and makes it my fault!"

In both of these cases, Lonny avoids two things. He talks about his past rather than his present, and he speaks to his thinking rather than his feelings. These are comfortable places for Lonny to go. Even though they aid him in avoiding his present experience, they are known quantities, thus safer in their own way. Encouraging and guiding Lonny towards being more present, as well as helping him to focus on and experience his feelings, will offer him the opportunity to see that there are different choices. More importantly, that his emotions and attending to his here-and-now life are experiences that he can survive. The more he can experience these choices as positive and healthy, the more he will make them on his own. They may not always be comfortable, but they will allow him to experience more of "who" he is and can be in the world.

*The Aesthetic/Ethical Split*

As discussed above, Lonny also appears to be stuck between the aesthetic and ethical levels of existence. If you remember from Chapter 3, the aesthetic level speaks to the natural developmental phase in which we are more self-centered and spontaneous. This is seen as a healthy part of our moral/values development in our earliest childhood, as we must first come to know ourselves prior to being able to relate to others. It is this self-knowledge that informs our understanding of others. In addition, this healthy narcissism allows us to build a strong enough sense of our potentiality that we can feel safe enough to transcend each moment in order to generate who we can become. From a more Zen perspective, it is what allows us to not be attached to a static "self," so that this ongoing process of unfolding potentiality can be realized. The ethical level of development is reflective of how we come to understand ourselves in relation to others and the world. In particular, the world of shared values and norms that brings forth the respect and valuing of the group and community in connection with the individual. In the healthiest of worlds, this is what tempers our "potentiality" from becoming an unhealthy and fixed "ego" by encouraging us to consider our relationality. Becoming stuck in or between either of these levels results in an inability to transcend our moments, to be unable to create ourselves anew.

For Lonny, this is evidenced by his tendency at times, to react to his neurotic anxiety from his younger, more narcissistic place. This is a sign of being stuck in the aesthetic. It shows up in ways in which he avoids his healthy anxiety by self-soothing behaviors, such as his abuse of alcohol. Abuse of substances is one example of how, being stuck in the aesthetic creates the illusion of having, and becoming attached to a static "self." He also, at times, moves into the ethical realm, in those instances when his anxiety is avoided by splitting into dualities. This shows up in symptoms where he is caught in there being a "right" or "wrong" answer, or a "good" or "bad" decision; a space in which the paradoxical nature of the world is too overwhelming. Particularly under stress, this tendency towards duality shows up. In sessions, it most often shows up the closer we are getting to his discomfort, whether it is touching on feelings (especially uncomfortable feelings), tension in his body or other somatic discomforts, or moving him closer to acknowledging his choice and subsequent responsibility. In this latter place, it often arose, as he became aware of how often he chooses not to choose, and the detrimental effects this has in his life.

## The Importance of Context

All of the above ways in which Lonny has come to live and survive in his world must always be understood within his contextual experience. How does Lonny's experience of being gay, white (specifically of German and Irish descent), male, an ex-Mormon, of middle class background, contribute to his understanding and experience of being in the world? How do these cultural influences along with his current middle class, urban lifestyle impact how he views his life? His interactions with his Umwelt, Eigenwelt, Mitwelt, and Überwelt? How will my own contextual experiences influence my understanding of Lonny and our work together? Beyond culture, what other contextual understandings must be attended to? How might the social, political, and environmental factors in our world also play a role? What about the relationship we form? The intersubjective experiences we have in our work together? These are questions that are critically important to consider if the therapeutic work is to progress, and if I want to create a safe and nurturing environment for growth and change. As our work unfolds, it is important that I bring to the relationship a willingness to ask the questions that will help us both to consider the role of culture and context.

## Attending to the Here-and-Now Experience

As has been stated several times earlier in this book, a major focus of any Existential practice is towards staying fully present in the here and now. Existential theory in general has a strong commitment to understanding temporal reality. That is to say, a belief that time is not a linear process, rather a process that happens concurrently on several levels. In more practical terms, there is an understanding that our history and our future are always unfolding in the present. As we make choices in our life, we are actively transcending each moment to create who we are and who we can become. This requires us to utilize our history to create our future. Often, however, we "forget" this innate capacity to transcend ourselves, and thus become locked into believing and acting as if our history defines our present and our future; or conversely, that our future will allow us to escape our past or our present. This ultimately winds up with our becoming stuck in our past or future, thus avoiding our present experience. By living in (and from) our past or future, we live reactive and out-of-balance lives, rather than living authentic and congruent lives in the present and from moment to moment. As a result, we avoid the healthy anxiety that propels us to transcend our here-and-now experience, and instead experience neurotic anxiety which binds us to a belief that we are our history or future, that we are a "self" that is doomed to never change.

For Lonny, living in the past was his way of survival for a period earlier in his life. However, as he became an adult, other options opened for him, yet he "chooses not to choose," rather to live his life as if it is already pre-determined by his history. As discussed earlier in this chapter, this showed up in counseling as responses to our work that consistently deflected from his here-and-now experience. His references were to "what was" rather than "what is." His tendency towards avoidance of feelings also served to strengthen his already out-of-balance reliance on his intellect. My work with Lonny over our time together was to try and keep him in the moment with me. The following examples of our work together will highlight ways in which our therapeutic work unfolded, utilizing myself as the predominant tool. Within this, I paid attention to how avoidance of his experience was projected into the room energetically, and how "naming" my observations and, more importantly, my experiences being with Lonny, became the impetus for his work to unfold.

### Clinician as "Tool"

Contextual Existential practice posits that rather than relying on a series of techniques meant to respond to certain specified symptoms or problems, the counselor/therapist him or herself is the most effective tool of clinical practice.

In addition, Contextual Existentialism understands the intrinsic value of the fact that we are relational beings, thus the power of healing happens within the relationship between client and clinician. Because existentialism as a whole understands that each person is unique, there can be no technique that is uniformly useful for a specific situation. Because most other western theories of psychology tend towards embracing the concept of "objectivity," it follows that they set forth a belief that one can determine a cause-effect relationship between "symptom" and "cure." Further, it is assumed that this "cure" is generalizable, that is to say, it will work in most, if not all, cases. This is not to say that interventions learned from other theories cannot be useful. In fact, Existential clinicians often "borrow" techniques from other theoretical perspectives. The difference is that these tools are used within an existential framework. They are used because *in the moment* they intuitively feel "right" for this client at this particular point in the work. This allows us to utilize the strength of the here-and-now relationship that calls forth the inter-subjectivity of our experiences as they happen, rather than fall prey to the fallacy of objectivity.

This takes us back to our understanding that to do work from an existential perspective means that the clinician must understand him/herself deeply, and must trust in her/his capacity to "listen" while with clients, and respond intuitively to what is happening in the moment. Thus the knowledge of what is happening in the moment between counselor/therapist and client comes through us, almost as if we are a conduit that the energy (knowledge) passes through, in order for us to see/hear/know it as it happens. If we do not take advantage of it as it happens, we miss an opportunity to guide our clients in what it means to live in the here and now. So, if in this present moment we experience an intuitive response that points us in the direction of a cognitive intervention, then so be it. Perhaps in that moment guiding the client to see his/her cognitive distortion is most useful. However, in another moment, that same scenario might move us to focus on the client's somatic or emotional experience. Or conversely, a similar scenario with a different client will most likely call forth a different intuitive response from the clinician. I believe it is crucial for counselors/therapists to take advantage of on-going education and training in a variety of intervention techniques. The more knowledge and experience we have, the better we can do our work. However, we must always understand that these "tools" become existential because of the intention with which we use them, and because of the Contextual Existential understanding that underlies their use.

In my work with Lonny, it is important that I stay fully aware of what is happening in the room. Because I know that my cognitive domain is strong, and in my own historical experience was over utilized as a coping mechanism, I must be very careful when working with clients who have similar histories. Although my reasons for over compensating in the cognitive were very different, it is easier for a client with this history to "hook" me, than one whom over utilizes their emotional, somatic, or spiritual domains. Fortunately for me, the kinesthetic is my strongest intuitive sense, thus it helps mitigate the energy of the cognitive more often than not. Still, being fully present and aware with Lonny is vital to our work. On more than one occasion I have found myself happily following him down the cognitive trail, waxing prolific about some intellectual understanding of our experience together. Suddenly, I realize that we have moved out of the present into the past (or sometimes, the future). At these moments it is important for me to acknowledge this to Lonny, and after we have worked together for awhile and built a level of intimacy, even to humorously point out to Lonny how good he is at moving us away from what was really going on. Usually, this is avoidance of his (and at times, my) anxiety in some form. Bringing us back to focus often moves me to pay more attention to asking him about his somatic and/or emotional experience as he tells his story. This brings the anxiety more into focus, and opens the door for Lonny to experience himself fully in the moment, even when this is uncomfortable. The more we can do this, the more Lonny can come to see that his anxiety will not destroy him, but that it actually can guide him towards choices that result in him experiencing his authenticity.

The importance of this example is to point out that how I came to the knowledge of what to do was by attending to my own experience of being with Lonny. Because I believe in the core concepts of Contextual Existentialism, I trust in the process and in my own capacity to be fully present. In addition, I hold implicit faith in the usefulness of my intuitive senses (the Intuitives), and in my ability to hold the container that allows Lonny to do his work. Perhaps the most important aspect of this work, is my capacity to be comfortable with "not knowing," to "letting go" of any need to have the answers for myself, or my client as we work together. We are on a mutual journey of exploration. That which needs to be known will reveal itself. If we are attentive to the moment-to-moment experience of ourselves, and our relationship, we will be able to attend to this "knowing" as it arises. In the next two sections of this chapter, I will share more specific examples of how this process of counseling/therapy unfolds through the mechanisms of transference and naming.

*Transference as Energy*

The concept of transference is common to all of the psycho-dynamically based theories of counseling and psychology. In most theoretical orientations, the transferential process includes both transference, the unconscious act by the client of projecting feelings about someone or something else onto their counselor/therapist and counter-transference, the unconscious act by the clinician of projecting feelings about someone or something else onto their client.

Within Contextual Existential theory and practice, transference and counter-transference are seen as two sides of the same coin, thus to divide them seems not useful. It does not really matter where the transference is coming from, rather that we are aware of the experience that arises from transference and make active use of it within the therapeutic process. Even more important, is the understanding that transference is an energetic process. Science, despite all of it's fallacies, has shown us that we are constant sources of energy, whether we speak of the electrical currents in the brain and nervous system, or in the heat that we give off from our bodies. Even our thoughts and dreams give off energy. Eastern medicine for centuries has been founded on the principles of energy and the focus on balance. It is not a stretch to understand that when we repress or deny aspects of our lived experience, we are not only repressing energy, but we are also using an enormous amount of energy to avoid our reality. Where does this energy go? From a psychological perspective, Contextual Existentialism would put forth first, that transference is more than just emotional projection, rather repressed feelings, body sensations, images, and thoughts; and second, these are projected out of the individual into the field around them. We all are picking up this projected energy in every moment. The healthier we are, physically and psychologically, the better able we are to allow that energy to pass through us. The less in balance we are, the more likely we are to pick up on some of this energy and to hold it as if it is our own. This adds to our imbalance, and can have profound effects on our physical and psychological well being. This includes our emotional and spiritual well being. When we are in a closer relationship with others, we tend to allow our natural defenses to this energy come down. This can leave us open and susceptible to any unwanted energy that is being projected. Particularly in our early development, we are vulnerable to this, and this speaks to why and how as children, and later as adults, we find our natural boundaries either too rigid or too permeable.

As stated above, the distinction between transference and counter-transference is artificial, and a product of a culture that values duality over paradox. The usefulness of this distinction is limited to a cognitive awareness of the source of the energetic projection. In other words, it is helpful to understand whether the energy being projected into our inter-subjective experience is a response to the clinician's versus the client's disowned experience. As counselors and therapists, it is crucial that we are able to identify this so that we do not use the client's counseling/therapy to work out our own issues. However, having said this, it is equally crucial not to discard this information completely. It has intrinsic value in our work with our client, as it does tell us something about our relationship. Not paying attention can result in us missing important and useful opportunities to explore our inter-subjective experience. What about my experience with the client evokes my own transferential process? What about my client's experience of me evokes his/her energetic projection?

In the case of Lonny, my experience being with him at times evoked a desire to take care of him, to in fact keep him safe from his emotional wounding. This clearly comes from my own historical experiences of care-taking others to avoid my own emotional pain. Yet, in our work together, being able to bring forth my experience into our work, with full acknowledgement that it was my experience (not his), allowed us to explore what in his here-and-now experience was being disowned into the room (energetically). In short, what part of him wanted to be "saved" from his uncomfortable feelings? In going back to the example raised earlier in the chapter, my getting caught in my "head" when with Lonny is another example of my own counter-transference. It connects directly to my own over utilization of my cognitive domain to avoid emotions. Yet, in naming this experience together, we can come to an understanding of how our individual experiences contribute to our inter-subjective experience, thus offering us opportunity to explore and examine the experience, and to bring ourselves into the here and now of it. This opens doors for the client (and myself) to engage with our authenticity.

## The Process of "Naming"

The concept of naming is really a very simple one. It is the act of sharing one's experience of what is happening from moment to moment within the therapeutic experience. It is one of the most powerful tools that a clinician can use when sitting with a client, and is often the precursor to any interventions. Yet, for many reasons it is often a difficult process, as it asks the counselor/therapist to not only be willing to share what they experience (see, feel, hear, intuit) going on with the client, even when uncomfortable, but also to share what they are aware of going on for themselves as they sit with the client. This often requires us to speak to our own most uncomfortable feelings and thoughts. We must be attending to our own blind spots, and attempting to sort through when our experience is truly one that is in response to the here-and-now moment within the therapeutic relationship, and not our own issues that have little to do with the person we are sitting with. Yet again, not discarding this completely, but using it to examine what, within our inter-subjective experience calls forth this response, and asking how it might inform us of the dynamics of this "present state" relationship. This brings us back to the chapter on assessment, sorting through what is our work versus the client's. Assessment is a moment-to-moment process, and in this way, is intricately connected to the use of naming.

One can see how the transferential process is often connected to the act of naming. As an energetic process, it often involves the projection of one's unwanted or unacknowledged feelings, thoughts, body sensations, etc. In certain cases, what the clinician might be experiencing with a client might be these energetic transferences, and thus naming this experience can help bring these into the client's awareness, and move them towards owning their own experience, and living more authentically in the moment. Of course, not all naming involves transferential energy. It is often a reflection back to the client of their body language, your awareness of your feelings or thoughts in relation to what has just been said or done, or even a theme that has arisen over several sessions or experiences.

One must understand that naming as a therapeutic tool is woven in the tapestry of the work. It is not just a technique that you use every once in awhile; rather it is the core of Contextual Existential practice. It requires the clinician to trust in the process and in his/her ability to fully engage in the moment with their client. It takes time and practice in order to utilize "self-as-tool" most effectively. Learning how to acknowledge your mistakes, and use them to move the work forward is integral. You are not the expert in your client's life! It is amazing how powerfully healing can occur when you can acknowledge your being human with your client. It allows them to see a real person, actively engaged in their own life. This gives them permission to be human, to make mistakes, learning to trust that you will not care for them any less, nor will you disappear from their lives because of it. It deepens the therapeutic process, allowing it to become the place where the client can practice being in a healthy relationship, both with themselves and with others; learning how to trust this enough to try it out in the rest of their lives.

With Lonny, as with all clients, there were always numerous opportunities to name what is happening within the here-and-now relationship. In one instance I might be noting how he has stopped breathing, or is breathing very shallowly. In another, I might name how his emotional and cognitive responses to me in a session, mirror his relationship with his partner, or his mother. It was not uncommon, particularly early in our work, but really at any time in which our work took us close to Lonny's feelings of fear or abandonment that he would try to figure out what he thought I wanted him to say or feel. I repeatedly would have to name this experience of him "care-taking" me or struggling to please me. I would not let him go there, not let him ignore his wishes and wants. In most cases, I would acknowledge the struggle and push him to name his own feelings and wishes. This often brought up intense anxiety early in our work, anger in the later stages. Learning to be with either the anxiety or anger opened him to experiencing himself more fully. At times, his out of awareness desire to avoid his feelings were so strong, that they were energetically projected into the room. I would experience sudden and intense feelings of fear, or anger, or frustration. They were clearly not mine, but would not be ignored. Thus, naming them moved them back into the energy field of our relationship, and helped Lonny to own them (at best), or to acknowledge and then repress them (at the least). Either way, it began to offer him a glimpse into an existence where his wishes and feelings had value and demanded attention. Within our relationship, he also began to experience what it meant to have someone honor his experience, even if his wishes and wants were not always met.

Naming the experiences in the room opened the door for other interventions as they arose. In the best of the work, interventions arose intuitively; seemingly coming into the room as if on their own, me being merely the conduit. I rarely knew what would come next, rather allowing myself to trust the knowledge as it showed itself. Equally, I would encourage Lonny to tell me what he needed to do next, or where the work needed to go. My direction came in helping him as he bumped up against his obstacles, freeing his river to flow naturally. It was his life, his river, and only he knew when to float and when to paddle. My attempts to be "pro-active" and second-guess the future were often my weakest moments, when interventions landed with a thud in the middle of the room. Not uncommonly, silence was my best friend in this work. If I was feeling a bit lost, chances are so was Lonny. Naming this experience for both of us freed us up to be open to what came next. Sitting in the quiet, whether for a moment or for many moments allowed room for the anxiety to reveal itself and propel our work forward. Being fully present is often experienced as sessions that unfold in an instant rather than in an hour. I came to understand that when I was conscious of time, I was not being fully present.

# Summary

In this chapter, we have learned how to take the information from our on-going process of assessment and utilize it to understand our client to the best of our ability. By trusting our capacity to sit with our client and pay attention to how their experience unfolds from moment to moment allows us to engage in the therapeutic process with integrity. By having faith in our capacity as humans to be fully aware, and trusting in our natural inclination towards homeostasis, we can "let go" of the need to know, and allow the experience to unfold, attending to our choices in each moment, and getting out of our own way. In believing that the client is the expert in his/her life, thus the navigator of their own destiny, we are freed from some false belief that we can somehow know what is right or wrong for them. Rather, we can guide them in accessing their own potential for creating themselves. We are facilitators of their process, the mid-wives of their birth and re-birth in each moment we are with them. By naming what is occurring in our relationship, including the transferential energy that is projected, we can move the process along, rather than get caught up in the neurotic anxiety itself. We can intuitively utilize interventions that, in that moment, are most effective. Finally, and most importantly, we can create opportunities for modeling our own authenticity, thus allowing our clients to experience all of their own potential to live an authentic and congruent life in all aspects of their being in the world.

# VIII

# Working with Couples

"If you gaze long into an abyss, the abyss will gaze back into you." Frederick Nietzsche


Because Contextual Existential theory by its nature is contextually oriented, the understanding of the intra-psychic world of the individual is always within a relational perspective. As such, it is an approach that is very conducive to working with couples or families. Rather than describing couple and family therapy as a systemic approach, one should understand that working with couples and families means understanding both the intra-psychic and inter-relational aspects for each member who is engaged in their work. Contrary to Whittaker's Experiential Family Therapy (Whitaker & Keith, 1981) and the work of Virginia Satir (Satir, 1967), both who have been influenced by existential theory, there is not an inherent belief that the system itself is the client, or that the system is necessarily the focus of the work. While most family systems theories are based on an understanding that the family is the most influential culture on the development of the individual, thus the intent of family therapy is to re-negotiate or re-orient the family system towards a healthier functioning; Contextual Existential theory understands that other forces are also at work in the development of the individual. There is an understanding that in any couple or family, each individual member brings a host of their own contextual experiences into the room and into the work, and that most often, those members who hold the most power also tend to have a proportionally larger impact on the functioning of the couple or family as a whole. Thus, while family roles certainly can be powerful forces, outside influences also impact how the individual situates him or herself within a family structure. Individuals are more than a product of their family of origin. We are equally influenced by larger systemic forces: friendships, society, culture, and the environment (both biological and artificial) in which we live, to name a few. Thus, each individual within a couple or family group brings in unique experiences and characteristics as a result. Working in the here and now, one must be able to address what emerges as it happens, whether that is clarifying an internal response or a relational one. Recognizing that any experience is always both an internal and relational process, the work is to understand, as best as one can, how a given issue is experienced in both arenas. It is particularly crucial to allow room for all participants in the therapeutic process to have equal voice.

In this chapter, as in Chapter 7, we will explore both the structure and content of the therapeutic interaction. Starting with the establishment of the therapeutic relationship, we will then focus on how one works within the "here and now," and the impact of this approach on both the clients and the clinician. By understanding the role of "clinician as tool" we will see how a variety of interventions might be utilized with a couple or family, inclusive of the role of transference and naming. More importantly, the necessity of including the whole person (both clinician and clients) in the movement towards homeostasis and authenticity will be examined. A case study of working with a couple will be used to bring to light how this process works when attending to both intrapsychic and systemic influences. It is to be understood that while more complex; similar dynamics would occur when working with a larger family structure, thus similar interventions would be utilized in our work.

# The Case of Peter and Rachel

Continuing with the use of Hays' ADDRESSING model (2001), let me introduce Peter and Rachel. Peter is a 32-year-old (A) heterosexual (S), white (of German and French descent) (E) male (G). His family has been in the U.S. (N) for several generations and is blue-collar working class (S). He grew up in Pittsburgh, Pennsylvania, where his family has lived for many years. Peter's generation was one of the first in his family to go to college, and he graduated with a degree in political science. He is employed as an assistant to a lobbyist for the lumber industry, and clearly has moved himself solidly into a more white-collar middle class experience. He has no physical or developmental disabilities (D, D), as well as no connections to indigenous cultures (I). He was raised Methodist (R), but is not currently actively involved in a church, although he does define himself as Christian.

Rachel is a 28-year-old (A), heterosexual (S), white (of Russian, Italian, and German descent) (E) female (G) whose family immigrated to the U.S. (N) during and after WWII. She was raised in an upper middle class background (S) going mostly to private girls' schools until college, when she "rebelled" and went to a state university. She also grew up on the east coast, where she met Peter in college. She comes from an Agnostic background (R), thus religion and spirituality were discussed from a philosophical and political point of view in her home, although her mother was raised Russian Orthodox in a middle class home. Her father came from money, but no formal religious background. Her parents are both university professors who decried formalized religious institutions, but were open to more eclectic spiritual traditions and explored Eastern mysticism as well as Sufi, Quaker, and Yoga approaches to life. Currently, like Peter, Rachel is not involved in any organized religious activity and describes herself as "spiritually curious." She too states no physical or developmental disabilities (D, D) and reports no Indigenous background (I). She is employed as a nurse, working in the intensive care unit of a local hospital.

A former client of mine referred Peter and Rachel to me. They entered counseling/therapy due to some struggles they were having over whether or not to have children. Rachel has a history of two miscarriages, and a part of the arguments that they are having are not only about trying to have children, but whether or not adoption is a choice. They currently live in a bedroom community of the city.

## Establishing the Therapeutic Container

As with Lonny in Chapter 7, I initially talked to Rachel and Peter on the phone. Although Rachel made the first phone call to me looking for an appointment, I asked to speak to both of them if possible to make sure that they were both willing to come in for the first evaluatory session, if they were going to pursue couples work. Both parties seemed quite committed to working on their problems, which was a wonderful indication of the possibilities that might lie ahead. We set up our first session. When working with couples, I will schedule a normal clinical "hour" for the evaluatory session, although I will encourage them to consider hour-and-a-half sessions for the remainder of our work if we decide to move ahead. My experience over time has been that one-hour is not enough when dealing with couples. One can barely get into the work and the time is up. However, I let the couple guide the decision, and if they choose an hour format, we will work with it, acknowledging the potential limitations, and with the understanding that we can extend time down the road if they request it, or if I feel the work is being compromised.

They came in on time, and we spent the usual time going over paperwork, and discussing my theoretical approach. They were fairly well informed of this already, since a friend of theirs who had worked with me in the past referred them. It was one of the reasons that they had called me. They felt that not only was communication a problem for them, but that they were dealing with issues of meaning in their individual and collective lives. I wanted to hear from each of them, what had brought them to this point of seeking counseling/therapy, and I wanted to give each of them an opportunity to let me know what they hoped would happen as a result. Again, as with Lonny, having a sense of their individual experiences and wishes and wants is crucial to doing Contextual Existential work. In addition, I wanted to observe them together, to begin to have some sense of how they are as a couple, not only verbally but also non-verbally, physically, and emotionally. In this initial, albeit short contact, I gained some inkling of their caring for each other through their willingness, even in discussing pain-

ful differences, to be in close physical contact. In addition, they were careful (respectful as opposed to tentative) in the language that they used, both about and
with each other. We scheduled on-going appointments, starting with an hour
format.

As I consider our future work together, I will again focus on creating a container that is safe and provides both of them an opportunity to reveal who they
are from moment to moment. Like individual counseling/therapy, my work will
be to understand them from their own contextual experiences, as well as the experience of our relationship together as it unfolds. The difference is that I need
to attend to both stories equally, as well as the story of their relationship as it re-
veals itself to me. Instead of the three energetic forces in the room with an individual client (the client, the clinician, and our relationship), we will have five
forces (each of the couple's individual energies, mine, the force of their relationship with each other, and our shared experience together). I will need to be even
more observant of my own responses and any transferential energy that may
emerge. The dance is a bit more complex, as we explore their individual intra-
psychic worlds, how they meet in their relationship, and the power of their (and
our) relationship itself.

## Foreground and Background

Remember that the concepts of foreground and background speak to the assessment information that you, as clinician, stay aware of as you work with your
client. Again, this includes the information that speaks to your own experience
in your life as well as when sitting with your client (the foreground), as well as
the questions you are quietly asking yourself to discern what is going on for
your client in their life (the background). The latter includes what paradox(es)
might be in the forefront, the predominant relational style, (in this case, styles),
and primary domains utilized. In addition, the background includes our understanding of the client's level of values development, and their ability (or not) to
stay in the present.

As I work with Peter and Rachel, I come to understand that while they both
spoke of finding meaning in their lives as part of what propelled them into coun-
seling/therapy, in fact, for Peter, the paradox of death/non-being and striving for
life seems most pronounced. His early concerns express an anxiety that seems
rooted in a need for his genetic continuation rather than out of a desire to have a
child. For Rachel, it appears more to be the paradox of isolation and desire for
connection, with symptoms of anxiety expressed around how she sees a child
contributing to a sense of "completeness" both in her relationship with Peter,
and with herself. Peter's anxiety seems to be evident mostly in relation to his
Eigenwelt (his inner world), while Rachel's seems more connected to her Mitwelt (her relational world). While on the whole, I see both Peter and Rachel as
less "stuck" in their anxieties (in other words, their symptoms, while of concern
to them, do not seem intractable), nonetheless, when anxiety does arise, they of-

ten find themselves overwhelmed. In addition, because their symptoms are coming from different sources, they often have difficulty understanding each other, or the thoughts and feelings of the other; thus communication grinds to a halt. This, for me, is an example of how communication issues in couples, while often seen as primary in therapy (Satir, 1988), is actually more truly a reflection of deeper discord that is a result of the very different contextual experiences of the parties involved. Of course, as was the case with Lonny in chapter 7, other paradoxes emerge as our work continues, but in the case of this couple, these remain the primary forces behind their dis-ease.

In terms of other assessment areas, Peter seems to have fostered a more detached style of relating, while Rachel is more aggressive. You can see how this might have an impact on their relationship! While Rachel seems to over-utilize her cognitive domain, Peter seems more stuck in his emotional domain. Neither of them seems very connected to their bodies. Both of them seem to be actively exploring the meaning making domain (that of the spirit), but struggle with processing at this level due to the "disconnects" they often experience in the less utilized domains in their lives. In terms of temporal reality, Peter future trips, while Rachel focuses on the past. Both of them seem to have some capacity to be in the moment, but this is newer for them and a place that is easily "forgotten" when stress and conflict arises, either intra or inter-personally. Finally, in relation to values development, both Peter and Rachel seem stuck between the ethical and the religio-spiritual levels. While both seem mostly to fluctuate evenly between the dualistic thinking of the ethical and the transcendent thinking of the religio-spiritual, interestingly enough, under more acute stress, Peter clearly favors the world of splitting into right/wrong and good/bad, while Rachel escapes into the transcendent experience losing all touch with her groundedness.

You hopefully are beginning to see how the complexity of working with a couple can impact and influence the work in counseling/therapy. It is one thing to focus in on the nuances of an individuals complex inner world, and quite another to attend to a myriad of energetic movements within the dance of intersubjectivity, not just between the client and clinician, but between the couple in this case. The remainder of this section of this chapter will go into more detail as to how both Rachel and Peter's dis-ease manifests, and then how this evidences itself in their relational experience. Suffice it to say, it becomes even more crucial that the clinician must closely attend to his or her own experience while working with a couple, as the opportunities for transference are more complex. Moving as fluidly as possible between the inner and outer worlds of all three people in the room becomes paramount.

### Death/Non-Being & Striving for Life and Detached Relational Style (Peter)

As with Lonny in the previous chapter, time spent with Peter and Rachel begins to weave a certain pattern in each of their lives and in their life together. As Peter tells his story, which most often starts with what is happening in his relationship with Rachel, but easily moves in the direction of following the strands

to his recent and historical experiences; it becomes clear that the paradox of
death/non-being and striving for life emerges. As Peter's story unfolds from session to session, the symptoms of his anxiety become clearer to me. Both he and
Rachel very much want to have children, and for Peter, the mis-carriages have
evoked a strong reaction in him. He reports decreases in his ability to sleep, increased nervousness which is having an impact on both his work and personal
life, and he reports several dreams that have left him unnerved. He describes his
feelings alternating between scared and anxious, and then numb. He is confused
as to why he is feeling this way, particularly because he realizes how much Rachel is also hurting, and he feels guilty for his reactions when she is the one who
has had the trauma of the mis-carriages (at least physically). Rachel often stops
him when he talks like this in session (and apparently outside of sessions as
well), reminding him that they are both in this together, and that she understands
that he feels badly as well. I ask him when this started, and he stops to consider
this. Rachel responds, stating that his agitation and distraction seemed to emerge
after her second mis-carriage (about eight months ago). Peter nods in agreement.
I then ask how he handled the first mis-carriage. Again, Rachel speaks up first,
noting that Peter was really "there for me," attentive to her needs. I note that she
seems to be answering for him, and again ask Peter what he remembers. He
seems contemplative at this point. After a moment or two, he finally says, "I
didn't really allow myself to feel anything. I focused completely on responding
to how Rachel was feeling. It was like it wasn't real. The mis-carriage did not
happen. Rachel just didn't feel well."

Nonetheless, Peter's confusion persists. He reports that his dreams are full
of images of being chased by some unknown person or force. He never sees who
is chasing him, but has emotional and visceral awareness that if caught, he could
die. When I asked Peter if these symptoms are familiar to him, he initially says
"no." However, with further gentle pressure, he remembers that he has had times
in his life where he had difficulty sleeping, and where this has had an impact on
his day-to-day life. He specifically can remember a time during his adolescence
when his parents were fighting and on the verge of separating. When asked how
he coped with this, he thought about it, and stated, "I decided to just ignore it,
pretend it wasn't happening. I focused on school work, and extra-curricular activities which kept me distracted"; "I convinced myself I didn't care, and, it
worked!" In this case, apparently the conflict subsided (Peter is not sure why, he
has never asked his parents about it, nor have they ever talked about it to their
children). Peter basically detached from the situation, and lucky for him, the external world cooperated. While I suspect that there are additional examples to be
found, this is enough to begin to help Peter see how he deals with stressful situations.

As we continue to work together, Peter begins to make connections between
how he responded when his parents were fighting, and how he responded when
Rachel had her first miscarriage. He sees that his initial reaction to conflict or
stress is to detach from his own experience (his own emotions in particular) and
to focus on something else (school, activities, Rachel). When the second miscar-

riage occurred, his emotions overwhelmed him, but he found it more difficult to detach completely. The result was a swing back and forth between cutting his emotions/experience off, and being flooded by them. His attempt at not feeling led to increased anxiety and thus the other disturbances (sleep disruption, dreams, etc.). Peter reports, and Rachel concurs, that when things in life are going well, Peter is very in touch with his emotions in general, and is a very empathic, caring husband and friend. He is the one that others come to talk to when things are rough; he is able to connect well emotionally to others. Rachel states that she thinks he gets too emotional at times. Peter smiles at this, but says he likes the fact that he is so in touch with his feelings. When I ask about why he thinks that he detaches from his feelings when he is afraid, Peter at first says, "I don't know." After reflecting for a moment or two, he then says he does the same thing when he gets angry. He cuts it off, and then wonders out loud if fear and anger are connected for him. I agree it is something to consider.

### Isolation/ Desire for Connection and Aggressive Relational Style (Rachel)

While we have spent some time exploring Peter's experience; it is important to remember that during sessions, I followed whatever emerged as we spent time together. There were some sessions where more time was spent on Peter, others on Rachel, and still others where the relationship itself was the main focus. Of course, since couple's counseling was the modality that we had agreed to, the work was always tied back to how it had an impact on the relationship. It was not uncommon that all three areas were touched on as they were all intricately entwined. For the sake of understanding their individual contextual experiences, it is useful here to focus on each one first, then come back to talk more about the ebb and flow of the work itself.

For Rachel, what emerged as we worked was her strong desire to feel "complete" (in her own words). When pressed further about this, she talked about how growing up in her family, despite her parents' strong independent streaks, her mother would talk to her about how when she met Rachel's father, she felt whole. Rachel witnessed how her parents, over the years, seemed to finish each other's sentences, to almost know what each other was thinking. This observation, combined with her mother's comments about feeling whole, had a strong impact on how Rachel, consciously or not, thought about herself. While she was raised to think that she could be anyone she wanted to be, and to do anything she wanted to do, there was an undercurrent of anxiety below the surface about not being complete until she met someone to live her life with. She was aware of this, and in our initial conversations seemed to think this was normal. It came as a shock to her when I questioned whether or not this was valid. Even Peter seemed surprised to hear this from her; especially that she had never mentioned this to him before. He told her that one of the reasons he was initially attracted to her, was her independent streak, and how she always "went after what she wanted, including me."

As we continued to explore this theme, it became clearer that underneath the exterior image she presented to the world, Rachel felt vulnerable and alone. "One of the things people don't know about me, is that I hate being alone. I will always find a way to fill my time up with other people. If I have to spend time alone, I usually distract myself by reading a book, watching a movie, or something else. I've gotten better at this, but I still have a sense of dread when I am alone and my time is not planned." This began to reveal more evidence of her relational style. Rachel, more often than not, initiated contact with friends, did the planning, took care of business, and, as Peter pointed out, "was like a barracuda when it comes to protecting what is hers . . . whether things or people or experiences." At other times in our work, Rachel spoke of the relief she experienced when she met Peter, of how happy she was when they got married. She had worried (secretly) prior to this if she would ever meet someone who would love her. While I did not broach the subject of the "I-It" relationship (Buber, 1970/1996) as a concept to consider when Rachel initially revealed this, at later sessions, it became an area of exploration for Rachel, both in relation to her marriage and her desire to have a child.

Either way, these revelations revealed a recurrent theme of anxiety produced from her experience of the isolation/connection paradox. It became a crucial ingredient in our work together and ultimately in the work of their relationship. At several points in our early sessions, I wondered aloud how this isolation anxiety was connected to her miscarriages, and her/their current dilemma about having a child. I wondered about the meaning that having a child had for Rachel. These questions initially provoked a certain level of defensiveness in Rachel. Her body would tighten, her fists would clench, but when I would notice this aloud, she seemed surprised. When I asked what she was feeling, she answered, "I don't know." With further probing, asking her to notice her somatic responses specifically, she began to be aware of the tightness of her muscles in her hands, her chest, and her throat. When asked to fully experience this tightness, she began to notice the anxiety that was held in the tension. Taking her to the next level of awareness, I asked what might she might experience if we could "strip away the anxiety . . . what might be beneath it?" I encouraged her to breathe, and as she did, she became aware of a level of fear. Asking her to stay with this feeling, she connected this fear to her earlier fear of being alone, and of not being whole.

We did this exploration over several sessions. Finally, at one point she turned around and looked at Peter and said, "Oh my god, I just realized that all this time, before I was pregnant, and even while I was pregnant, my image was always of the three of us making up the perfect family. It was like a picture postcard. It could have been any three people, not necessarily you and I and our baby. It was the *idea* of having a family more than it being *our* family. It was about me feeling whole and happy no matter what. It was about what it was *supposed* to be, not whether or not you or I wanted it." I helped Peter and Rachel process through this information, especially working with Rachel to understand that this was her neurotic anxiety based on her past experiences, and not reflective of whom she was as a person, or who she could become. Peter was wonderful and caring, *and with help* was also able to own his disappointment. With further work, which I will discuss a bit later, they began the process of exploring who they wanted to be and how to move in that direction.

*Living in His (Peter's) Emotions and in the Future*

As stated earlier, Peter seemed to be over-compensating in his emotional domain, and while he actively engaged with his cognitive domain, and to a degree, his spiritual/meaning-making domain, he seemed fairly out of touch with his somatic experience. In addition, he lived his life in the future. As we worked, it became clearer how much time he spent focusing on what was to happen next. He tended towards scheduling his life so that the next days, weeks, and months were (mostly) clearly defined. When asked about this, he described his hectic work life, with meetings and travel, especially when congress was in session. So, to a degree, his need to schedule made practical sense. However, as our conversations unfolded over time, his pattern around scheduling also began to reveal his attempt at orderliness as a means to control his environment, and ultimately to reduce his own often disowned anxiety. When I would ask him to pay attention to his here-and-now experience, he would look confused, and he would fidget in his chair. He would have a similar reaction if I asked him, "What would it be like to not have your entire day/week/month scheduled?" I kept bringing him back to his present experience, to his body primarily. At first, he had difficulty staying with his somatic sensations, and would often allow himself to be distracted (look out the window, change the topic, or just "go away"). Gradually, with support, he could stay present for longer periods and he was able to begin to explore what these in-the-moment experiences were about for him.

Peter began to slowly understand that by attempting to control his external world, he was trying to feel safer in his internal world, where, for a variety of reasons, including his earlier life experiences, he often had felt unsafe. The deeper he was able to go into his present experiences, the more he understood how closely tied his concern about feeling safe was to a deeper anxiety about existing at all. His life experiences had been filled with periods of uncertainty, not only about what might happen *around* him, but what might happen *to* him. On some level, these experiences called into question who he was and how he fit into the world. These were questions of his *being-ness*. It began to make sense of his attempt to control his world by projecting into the future a false sense of certainty (if I see on my schedule that I have things to do, places to go, people to interact with for the next few days/weeks/months; then I have a reason to be and will exist into the future). He also was able to make links to how Rachel's miscarriages threatened this "planned future" and called into question his own existence. Yet, there was one more interesting layer that exposed itself to us as we worked.

Much later in our time together, Peter came to a session one day with a "powerful and very scary dream." He related that in this dream, he was once again experiencing being chased. As usual, he could not see who was chasing him, and he had no understanding of why he was being chased, but he knew that if caught, he would die. Usually Peter wakes up just as he is about to be caught. This time, however, Peter notices that "the unknown force chasing me is clearly getting closer. I can almost feel it breathing down my neck" (note that the force is an "it"). "This time, instead of waking up, I become aware of some force ahead of me; a force that is not frightening to me, rather it is comforting. I somehow am able to find energy to push forward, to gain distance between myself and the evil force behind me. It is almost as if I am being pulled forward. As I run, I see a little boy ahead of me, calling to me, telling me I will be OK. That's when I wake up this time."

I ask Peter if he is willing to re-tell the dream. He agrees. Using a gestalt dream work approach, I ask him to close his eyes, and re-live the dream in this moment as much as possible. I stop him at points during the re-telling of the dream to ask him to take on different aspects of the dream; the evil "it," himself, the dark, and ultimately the little boy. I ask him what he is experiencing in this moment in each of these roles (understanding that each part of his dream is a part of himself). I ask him to describe what he is aware of, his thoughts, his feelings, and his body. I ask what the meaning and purpose is of each aspect of his dream self. Noticing some anxiety as he works at staying present for this process, Peter is able to describe his experiences fairly well, and he has a series of insights as to the meaning of this dream for himself. He notes how the dark force is his life, and his awareness that it is speeding by and will end one day. He connects once again to something he had become aware of in an earlier session, how being "himself" in this dream was an experience of how he often kept his fear of not existing out of his conscious awareness, "running through life in fear, fear of not knowing who I am, and yet not knowing why or how to fix it." He experiences being the dark itself, and connects it to his habit of detaching and not being present when life gets difficult. Finally, he sees the boy as the part of himself that knows that he exists and will be OK, and simultaneously, he turns to Rachel and exclaims, "He is also our child who will allow me to live on through him." Peter is very present at this moment, and begins to tear up. When I ask him to stay with this, he is able to do so, perhaps for the first time without much of a struggle. When I ask him to put words to his tears, he states that he realizes that having a child was a way to avoid his own fear of not existing, both figuratively and literally. I note to him that this is an example of an "I-It" relationship, a concept I had introduced to both of them several sessions earlier. He was able to see this (as was Rachel, but more of that later).

This was a difficult yet powerful session for both Peter and Rachel. While the focus was on Peter, Rachel was clearly there with him, and I could see that she was having responses to this as well. In some ways, it was a mini-crisis point for Peter. He was forced to call into question his whole reason for wanting a child, while simultaneously becoming very clear as to why he had such a strong reaction to Rachel's miscarriages. I reminded him (and them) that this was also an opportunity to work on the meaning level that they both had expressed interests in exploring.

*Living in Her (Rachel's) Head and in the Past*

For Rachel, it could be said that "safety" was equated with "having the answers." From the beginning, and as our work progressed, Rachel was a clear presence in the therapy room. While Peter was, more often than not, comfortable with sitting in silence, or in pondering his emotional experience, Rachel rarely allowed for such moments. As noted earlier in this chapter, Rachel would often answer for Peter if he took too long, and if the focus was on Rachel, she would hardly ever leave room for a moment of silence or contemplation. When such moments occurred, she would physically react by fidgeting in her chair, tapping her foot, adjusting her clothes or hair. Initially she would become defensive if this was noted to her, or if able to hear me share what I saw, would quickly come up with a "logical" answer as to why she was doing whatever it was she was doing. It took many sessions, including ones where she was able to see Peter struggle in the quiet in order to make sense of his experiences, before she was willing to even try to attend to her here-and-now experience in the room.

In one particular session, the discussion had been on the ways each of them had coped with the second mis-carriage. Peter had come to a revelation about his avoidance of his own anxiety and fear, and how having a child was a wish fulfillment based more on his own needs than that of either his wife or child. As attention turned to Rachel, her first response was a quick and witty, "Well, I'd already had one mis-carriage, so I knew what was going on, and what to do." After some prodding and a startled look from Peter, she continued, "Of course I was sad, but at that point, being sad wasn't going to change the situation. I wanted to know why this had happened to me again." I noticed out loud that it seemed that in that moment, she was more interested in figuring out the "why's" of it all, rather than allowing herself to feel her grief (and perhaps other feelings as well). Rachel seemed confused, and wondered out loud what good feeling sad would do. Peter responded by asking her if it bothered her that he felt so sad. She said, "No, but it still doesn't change anything, and it certainly doesn't answer the question, 'Why?'" Again, I noted how important it seemed that Rachel "know" the reason for her mis-carriage, and I asked if she would be willing to try something in that moment. She looked a bit dubious, but agreed.

I ask her to stop, take a few deep breaths, and to just notice what she is aware of, in her body, in her feelings, in anything else that is in her awareness. She looks a bit perplexed, but takes a couple of fairly shallow breaths and sits there. I stop her, and again ask her to take some deep breaths and this time to close her eyes, and tell me what she notices. I help her to relax by focusing her breaths and paying specific attention to her body. She is able to notice some tension and tightness in her abdomen, her groin, and her thighs. I ask her to focus her breathing into those areas, to imagine that each breath helps to loosen the tension and to relax the muscles. With support, she is able to do this, and as I continue to both support her and ask her about what she is experiencing, she slowly begins to report noticing that as each of these areas of tension relaxes, she notices warmth spreading throughout her abdomen in particular. I ask her to pay attention to this area, and this sensation of warmth, and to notice anything else. She then becomes aware of an image of a dark, round ball sitting in the center of her abdomen. When I ask if it has any particular features, she says it is small, very heavy, and very hard. I ask what purpose it has, and after a moment, she tilts her head to one side, and her mouth seems to form an "O." Then, she shifts a bit in her chair, and opens her eyes. She looks at Peter, and then me. When I ask her what is happening, she says, "Oh, it's nothing," then adds, "I had the most curious sensation that the ball was me."

"Say more," I ask. She shifts again in her chair, and quickly says, "Oh, it doesn't matter, it's nothing really." She seems a bit uncomfortable, which I note out loud to her. "Well," she says, "What does it matter, it's just some image in my mind . . . it's probably nothing. Besides, what does this have to do with anything?" I suggest that perhaps her experience with both the images and the sensations presented themselves for a reason; that while it is true we can always make things up, that such visual and kinesthetic metaphors can actually help us understand confusing aspects of our life, our lived experience. I ask her to just "humor me" for a bit longer. She agrees, so I again ask her to close her eyes, take a breath, and notice if she could still see or sense this hard, dark ball in her abdomen. She could, so I ask her to just "be with it for a moment or two, and let yourself just observe whatever comes up." As she sits there, I encourage her to put into words whatever comes up; images, feelings, sensations, words. "Allow yourself to be the ball. What is your purpose?" She sits again for a minute or so, then says "to distract, to take up space." "To distract from what?" I ask. "From feeling," she says, "from feeling scared and angry." She opens her eyes and looks at me. "The ball is hard and heavy, but hollow. Hard on the outside, and so heavy that I can't even pick it up or carry it. So all of my attention is on how hard and heavy it is, but not on what is inside, or what might happen if I drop it. I've given up on things being different, rather assuming that this is how it always will be."

We were almost done with the session that day, but I asked Rachel to just take what had happened with her, and allow herself to consider it if it came up during the week. We would come back to it many times over the course of our work together. For Rachel, it was the beginning of her ability to see that by focusing so much on "figuring things out," she was able to avoid having to deal with her feelings, or for that matter, some elements of her somatic experience.

## The Ethical/Religio-Spiritual Split

As noted earlier in this chapter, both Peter and Rachel seem to be stuck between the ethical and religio-spiritual levels. In a developmental sense, the ethical level describes the place where the individual meets the group; where finding a balance between personal versus collective wishes and wants are explored.

This is the domain of rules, morals, and values; whether it is dictated by society at large, the family, or an institution like religion or politics. The religio-spiritual level describes the domain of the transcendent, whether described in secular or spiritual terms. This is the domain where, to paraphrase Kierkegaard (1954/1986), "one must, at times, rise above the group." To move into the religio-spiritual domain, one becomes clearer and more comfortable with one's own authenticity so that one is not attached either to one's own narcissism, or to the mindlessness of the group. From a Zen perspective, this reflects the desire for non-attachment, so that it is not one's ego that is driving choices, but rather choosing towards authenticity, towards actions and choices reflecting core beliefs and values, even when they are in opposition to the group. This can be a difficult realm to navigate, as it requires one to have worked with intentionality on oneself; to have spent time in self-reflection and exploration of the parameters of self-in relationship.

While both Rachel and Peter struggle to move fluidly between the three levels of development, most noticeably between the ethical and religio-spiritual, how their respective symptoms manifest when they get "stuck" between these last two levels, is markedly different. When Peter gets stuck, his anxiety shows itself in behavior that is firmly planted in the ethical domain. His world becomes one that is dualistic, where things are "either/or" rather than "both/and." It is in this place that he loses his ability to hold the tension of his experience, and instead splits into such polarities as "good/bad" or "right/wrong." His attempt to control his world becomes a battle where losing equates to not existing. In the case of having a child, while Peter can be incredibly supportive and caring to Rachel in response to her miscarriages, on another level, he has internalized the experience to "having failed." His fear of not having a child becomes evidence of his failure, his "not OK-ness." Despite the fact that there are no clear understandings as to why Rachel has miscarried, Peter's tendency is to assume there is something wrong with him. This shows up as our conversations unfold, and Peter becomes even more aware of how focusing his time and attention on Rachel allows him to avoid his own fear and anxiety, which results in the symptoms of his nightmares, the shutting down of his feelings, and his constant struggles to keep his world in perfect order.

Rachel, on the other hand, has a tendency to "escape" to a transcendent place when her anxiety rears its head. While true transcendence from the ethical to the religio-spiritual is evidence of a movement towards authenticity, using transcendence to avoid anxiety shows up more as a way to not face one's authenticity. One excellent example for Rachel is in how she chooses to act as if her miscarriages carry no real import, except in the clinical sense. Her desire to "know" (intellectually) *why* she miscarried masks her fear of the experience itself, thus a way to avoid having to feel her feelings or to be in her body. She successful detaches from both of these realms.

Another way that demonstrates Rachel's avoidance of anxiety through "pseudo-transcendence" shows itself during one session in particular when we were exploring how each of them made meaning in their lives. Peter had instigated this discussion in response to a previously discussed "a-ha" moment when he saw how his desire for a child was, in no small way, a desire to "live on through offspring" (Yalom, 1980), in other words, a way to avoid his own death anxiety. This brought up issues of spiritual beliefs for both of them. While Peter was more open and willing to move into an exploration of his anxiety in this paradox, Rachel became extremely uncomfortable. She became argumentative with Peter as he explored his own discomfort, using language like "when I get anxious I just put my trust in something greater than myself. I know it will all work out." When pressed to discuss what might happen if she were to face and explore her anxiety, rather than "turn it all over to some greater power," she became even visibly more uncomfortable. In this space, she had detached from both her feelings and her body. When one has explored their beliefs and values with intentionality, letting go of one's own ego or groupthink, a move into the religio-spiritual is a holistic experience, where one can stay present with all of their domains, and with fluidity can identify clear choices and subsequent consequences. It is a place of ultimate calmness, not of avoidance. There is no need to argue or defend one's position or experience. This was not the case with Rachel during this particular discussion.

As we continued our work together, and as more time passed, both Peter and Rachel began to understand how they individually dealt with their anxiety, and how their ability to transcend successfully between the ethical and religio-spiritual domains was compromised. While Peter was able to explore and navigate this more easily in our work, Rachel did come to a place where she was able to see how she got in her own way in this area, and while she still tended to miss it when it happened more often than not, she did become more conscious. This was a good start. It also proved helpful to do this work together, so that each of them could be supportive of the other as they struggled in moving more fluidly between the three domains of this developmental process.

## The Importance of Context

As was the case in the previous chapter (working with Lonny), here too, we must always understand Rachel and Peter's experiences in the context of their lives, both as individuals, and within their relationship together. How do their respective historical and current cultural factors contribute to their understanding and experience of being in the world? How do these cultural influences impact how each of them views their lives, separately and together? While each of them has interactions with their Umwelt, Eigenwelt, Mitwelt, and Überwelt, is there a way in which their relationship also takes on these four worlds? As with Lonny, how will my own contextual experiences influence my understanding of Peter, Rachel, their relationship, and our work together? Beyond culture, what other contextual understandings must be attended to? How might the social, political, and environmental factors in our world also play a role? What about the relationship we form? The inter-subjective experiences we have in our work together? Once again these are questions that are critically important to consider if the therapeutic work is to progress, and if I want to create a safe and nurturing environment for growth and change. As our work unfolds, it is important that I bring to the relationship a willingness to ask the questions that will help us all consider the role of culture and context.

## The Here-and-Now Experience

Once again, we are reminded that staying in the present is our goal, and a way for us all to live more authentic and congruent lives. As was discussed in the previous chapter, understanding that the past and future are always contained in the present is one way to try to grasp the significance of a present focus. This again is an example of how western existential philosophy and psychology shares an important insight with Buddhist thinking regarding the nature of health, the mind, and the impermanence of our existence. To focus on the past or the future, at the expense of the present moment, moves us towards a false sense of "self," and as a result, increases our neurotic anxiety and the accompanying symptoms of dis-ease. For Peter, his tendencies towards living in the future allowed him an escape, as he focused more on what he wanted to happen and who he hoped to be, he missed who he was in the moment (and from moment to moment). This keeps him from experiencing his lived experience as it happens, which ultimately gets in the way of integrating these experiences and moving him forward in his life. Driven by his fears of not existing, of truly being "nothing," escape to the future gave him a false sense of being. Unfortunately, until Peter began to allow himself to experience himself in the moment, as he truly was, his experience of existence was like a hollow shell, built on a fantasy of who and how he hoped to be. Likewise, for Rachel, living more in her past kept her focused on all that was missed or failed in her life. It is like she was continuously defining her self based on her historical experiences, while simultaneously running from it. For her too, her here-and-now experience, complete with the healthy anxiety that comes with it, was more often than not missed in her constant habit of looking backwards. When one runs backwards with a focus on what is past, one misses the present until it too, has gone by.

*Therapist as "Tool"*

As noted in previous chapters, it is the therapist her/himself who is the primary "tool" of the therapeutic encounter. Rather than relying on a prescribed set of techniques for specific symptoms, it is incumbent upon the clinician to pay attention to what is emerging in the here-and-now experience, and to allow this information to indicate how the encounter will unfold. It is through this use of "self-as-tool" that "techniques" will emerge, whether the use of established techniques common in other theoretical approaches (but used, of course, with existential intention) or spontaneous and creative interventions that emerge through attention to one's intuitive experience.

As I worked with Rachel and Peter, it was important that I stay fully aware of what was happening in the room. Again, knowing that my cognitive domain is strong, I had to pay attention to the potential to get "hooked," particularly with Rachel, who also tended to get stuck in her head. Since the kinesthetic is my strongest intuitive sense, it was an effective tool in my work with both Peter and Rachel; with Rachel because it was helpful in taking her out of her intellect and slowly but surely into her body and emotions. With Peter, who was most often stuck in his emotional domain, the use of the kinesthetic helped him move from affective awareness to the body, then to making sense of his experience in the cognitive domain. In each of these therapeutic moments, it brings the anxiety more into focus, and allow for both Rachel and Peter to experience themselves fully in the moment, even when this is uncomfortable. The use of somatically oriented techniques like breath work, paradoxical intention, and even Gestalt dream work were effective tools in guiding them and their relationship towards a more holistic experience of being in the world (and with each other).

*Transference as Energy*

As noted in Chapter 7, it is crucial that we are able to identify the transferential process so that we do not use the client's counseling/therapy to work out our own issues. However, having said this, it is equally crucial not to discard this information completely. It has intrinsic value in our work with our client, as it does tell us something about our relationship. Not paying attention can result in us missing important and useful opportunities to explore our inter-subjective experience. What about my experience with the client evokes my own transferential process? What about my client's experience of me evokes his/her energetic projection?

In the case of Peter and Rachel, my experience being with them as individuals and a couple; and of course, in relationship with me, was full of transferential energy. My "counter"transference was most notable with Rachel in those sessions where the work was to guide her out of her cognitive and into her emotions and body. As someone who is easily seduced into my head, I found Rachel a master at enticing me into often stimulating, but avoidant conversations (sometimes debates) about the "why" of her (and our) experience. With Peter, the seduction was his focus on the future. I too am guilty of "future-tripping" as a way to avoid the anxiety (and experience) of the moment. It was easy for me to move into "planning mode" rather than to stay focused on the current experience, no matter how unpleasant. I have been doing this work for well over 20 years, so it is easier for me to catch myself and correct the direction of the session when these moments of distraction occur. I can imagine (and remember) how difficult it was to stay focused and in the present during many sessions earlier in my career!

*The Process of "Naming"*

Again, as noted in the previous chapter, "naming" is one of the most powerful tools that a clinician can use when sitting with a client. The dance is between attending to our own blind spots, and attempting to sort through when our experience is truly one that is in response to the here-and-now moment within the therapeutic relationship, and not discarding this completely, but using it to examine what, within our inter-subjective experience calls forth this response, and asking how it might inform us of the dynamics of this "present state" relationship. Naming is an aspect of the moment-to-moment assessment process as previously discussed in earlier chapters.

In the case of Rachel and Peter, as with all clients, there were always numerous opportunities to name what is happening within the here and now relationship. Whether I was interacting with them individually or as a couple, it was imperative that I paid close attention to what I was seeing, hearing, and experiencing (intuitively and otherwise) and to use this information as a therapeutic tool. Noticing to Rachel when she was stuck in her head, when she "went away" as I attempted to move her into her emotions or body, how she tried to avoid "experiencing" by asking "why," how she objectified the "other" in her life (whether Peter or the unborn child) in order to avoid the anxiety of not knowing herself; these were all effective opportunities to name my observations, the disowned emotions in the room, and the somatic sensations in my own body that I knew were not mine to hold.

With Peter, examples of naming included the opportunities to acknowledge the deep sadness and fear (and sometimes anger) that was often "hanging" in the room when he was unwilling to acknowledge them in himself. Naming also included noticing his tendency to "future-trip" as a way to avoid his here and now experience, his care-taking tendencies as a means to avoid self-care, and how getting lost in his emotions allowed him to avoid making difficult choices or making sense of uncomfortable experiences. As a couple, naming was a hugely important tool in helping them to see how their communication was often unidimensional; in other words, they often talked around and over each other, but rarely to each other. In this, they also worked off of assumptions about each other and their individual experiences in the world, rather than taking the time to stop and check in with each other to insure that what was being said was being heard, and vice versa.

Like with Lonny in the previous chapter, naming the experiences in the room opened the door for other interventions as they arose, more often than not intuitively and sometimes unexpectedly. Any attempts to be directive were usually a result of my own anxiety of "not knowing" and thus failed miserably. Silence again was my best friend in this work. Being able to acknowledge my being in a fog, my desire to "go away," my discomfort with "not knowing" was more often than not a sign of transferential energy being projected into the liminal space in our therapeutic relationship. Naming this experience for all of us freed us up to be open to what came next. Sitting in the quiet, whether for a moment or for many moments allowed room for the anxiety to reveal itself and propel our work forward. Once again, this is that example of temporal reality; that time is not linear and rarely experienced the same for all parties present. One session that seems to speed by for me, might be experienced as "taking forever" for Rachel and/or Peter.

# Summary

In this chapter, we have learned how to translate the energetic process of counseling and therapy from the individual domain to one that incorporates a family system. We can see how we go from dealing with three energetic forces in individual counseling/therapy (the clients, the clinicians, and the therapeutic relationship) to, in the case of a couple, five forces (each of the couples, the clinicians, the couple's relational energy, and the therapeutic relationship between the couple and the clinician). While not explicitly discussing a family systems orientation in our understanding the causal factors in the issues of this couple, implicitly we have seen how a Contextual Existential orientation to couples work is by its very nature, attending to a systemic understanding of the world. By the very fact that we are all beings-in-relation (and not only to other human beings, but to our natural world), one cannot do effective couples counseling/therapy *without* taking into consideration the myriad of relational/systemic/contextual factors that contribute to our experiences, and our understanding of our experiences. Ultimately, the learning is that we must be very intentional in our attention to the energetic forces in the room when doing therapy with more than one person, especially when dealing with a relational system. Not doing so, can leave us open to not only missing important information, but also in the risk of colluding with one party over the others, especially if we are not aware of our own transferential issues.

# Afterward (and AfterWords)

"And the day came when the risk to remain tight in a bud was more painful than the risk it took to blossom"—Anais Nin

I have chosen to call this the "Afterward" rather than the "Afterword" or "Chapter 9," mostly because I think it is a fitting way to end this book. What are the words, ideas, images that we have after having sat with our clients? How do we come to understand our experience of the work that has just occurred? How do we provide continuity of care with clients when our work is so focused on the here-and-now that we tend not to be note takers or documenters of history? This "Afterward" will focus on the work we do as clinicians in attending to our understanding of our clients and ourselves, once the sessions are over. The "AfterWords" are a suggested way of attending to what we have come to know in these realms, and as a way of providing this continuity that can be so important to our on-going work.

## The Clinician's Journal

In many counseling and therapy environments, the use of case notes is the common practice. A client file is established with demographic information, intake and assessment information, a formal treatment plan, and session-by-session notes on the client's work and the clinician's impressions of the work. This, in fact, may be a requirement, especially if you work in an agency setting. For licensed mental health professionals, most jurisdictions do require some level of documentation, although dependent on a clinician's theoretical/philosophical approach, what is documented can vary. At the least, most jurisdictions want basic demographic and financial records to be kept.

As a Contextual Existential practitioner, the focus is on avoiding freezing our clients in time, and in working in the here-and-now. As such, taking notes in the session, while not impossible, is discouraged in that it can easily distract the clinician from attending to what is unfolding in the room. In addition, keeping session notes that focus too heavily on what the client is dealing with in that particular meeting, can result in a tendency towards losing touch with the unfolding quality of existence, and again, freeze an image or construct of your client. Session notes become a comparison in a way, of seeing and understanding your client as some series of snapshots instead of a continuous flow of lived experiences.

Earlier in this book, I introduced the concept of Contextual Existential assessment as a tool for a here-and-now understanding of your client in the moment while simultaneously (and paradoxically) being curious about any themes or patterns that seem to emerge in their lives. This paradoxical approach to both seeing your client in the moment while also attending to any themes or patterns that emerge over time, is useful in that it allows us to choose how we work with the client in ways that systemically encompass both their present struggle and any over-arching pattern of concern. While I encourage a simultaneous awareness of *foreground and background* while sitting with the client, I am also proposing that one way to provide continuity of care for your client is by considering the *foreground* (your experience sitting with the client) as a tool for documenting your sessions with your clients once the session is over. This Clinician's Journal is not a "session note" of what the client reported or how they are progressing on some goal set in their initial contact, thus not anything that needs to go into a client's file. Rather, it is the clinician's own record of her/his experience and understanding of what it was like to sit with the client in that session. While you can utilize some of what comes from this process to do case notes if necessary, The Clinicians Journal offers a way to process *your* experience, *your* understanding of what unfolded, in order to help you see what worked (or not) and what role transferential energy played in the encounter. Ultimately, by following the assessment guidelines from the *foreground* of your work with your client, you will be able to gain a deeper and more useful understanding of the inter-subjective experience of the counseling/therapy process. This can prove invaluable to your work with your clients, as well as a tool for work with your own supervisor or consultant about your cases.

# Illuminata

Using a Clinician's Journal is a way of gaining a series of illuminations, what I term *illuminata*, about your work. Using the *foreground* as a template for dwelling on the experience of *being-with* your client, here are some examples of what can emerge when utilizing this tool. I am using a variety of cases to pull from:

**How present was I? How well was I able to stay in the here and now with my client?**

*It was really difficult to stay present with J. today. I found myself following him as he talked about what happened yesterday, last week, last month and avoiding what was being experienced in the moment as he told his stories. I was so captivated by the stories that I didn't stop and ask him to pay attention to what he was feeling, sensing, knowing as he told the story to me! J. was good!! He successfully kept me from the present. I felt lulled into a trance like state by his storytelling.*

*The session today with M. was intense but felt very productive. Time was irrelevant and the session seemed to fly by. I was aware of how focused and present I was as the session unfolded. M. was so in her body and in her feelings that my work was only to be with her, to support her process as she explored her anger and confusion about her relationship with her father*

*S. was late today by about ten minutes. She came flying in the door and started talking about what else she had to do before the day was done. I found myself responding more to her anxiety about "not enough time" than to her experience of herself in this anxiety. It took me about five minutes to bring her back to the present. Once there she was able to attend to her here-and-now experience more fully, and to begin to understand what was at the core of her anxiety.*

**How did I help the client stay in the here and now?**

*J. was so successful today with past-tripping that I did not do a very good job at all of helping him stay in the present. Instead, I tended to follow him into his past and get lulled into the content of his stories rather than what these stories were revealing about his here-and-now experience. It was not until the session was almost over that I realized how not present both of us were. I did make note of it out loud, and joked with him about how good he was at deflecting himself (and me) from what was really going on.*

*M. was so very present today that I did not have to do too much in this regard. This is not the usual when working with her, but I do feel it was indicative of how far she has progressed in being at ease with herself, especially with her feelings. My best tool today was my ability to sit with her in her discomfort and to encourage her to notice how her feelings of anger and confusion allowed her to begin to make sense of her experience of living with her father. It especially allowed her to begin to see how little he really sees and hears her, who she is in the world and what she wants.*

*Once I was able to slow S. down by asking her to stop talking and to close her eyes and breathe deeply, she was able to pay more attention to what was going on in the moment, and was less focused on what else she had to do that day. It was a struggle throughout the session, as her anxiety was so palpable in the room, but I used some meditative tech-*

*niques to help her stay present. This allowed her to tap into what was
going on for her, and to especially begin to see how her struggle with
time is thematic and a way for her to not be in touch with her experience of herself in any given moment.*

**What was I experiencing as I sat with the client? What did I notice
about my experience Somatically? Emotionally? Cognitively? Spiritually?**

*In my work with J. today, since I was not very present for most of the
session, I was not as aware of my own experience as I would want to
be. I was really in my head most of the time; right there along with J.
Since I know this is my own tendency when under stress or avoiding my
own life, this is no surprise. It is another reminder of how important it
is for me to stay attentive to J. in his process. He so avoids his experience of his emotions, but usually I can guide him towards body awareness, which eventually allows him to experience his feelings, even if
only for a moment. Today I was a talking head!*

*Sitting with M. today, I felt so focused and present! Most often, I could
feel a mixture of anger and fear, especially when she tried to disown
these feelings in herself. At times, I felt pressure in my stomach, like a
hard knot twisting inside my guts. When I noted this aloud to M., my
knot disappeared, as she was able to acknowledge her own sense of
tension in her gut. When M. talked about her father, I felt myself detach
even as I noticed to her that she was telling me about a painful conversation with him, yet in the room with me her voice had no affect?*

*For the first part of the session with S., I felt like there was not enough
oxygen in the room for either of us! Once I was able to ask S. to stop
and breathe deeply, it seemed like the room opened up and there was
more air. Every time S. started to future-trip about all of the chores and
appointments she still had to complete, I could feel my breathing getting shallow, and my head getting foggy. Noticing this out loud to her
really shifted the energy back to that space between us, and allowed S.
to come back into her here-and-now experience, no matter how scary.*

**What is my primary intuitive sense (visual, auditory, kinesthetic,
olfactory, gustatory)? How did it help guide me in this session?**

*I am predominantly kinesthetic, followed by visual. With my work with
J. today, I did not pay attention to my somatic experience very well until towards the end of the session when I realized how in my head I was.
As soon as I noted this out loud to J., I became acutely aware of how
tense my body was, and how detached my head felt from my body. I did*

*not have visual images today, but that is not as common working with J. as is my usual awareness of my somatic experience when sitting with him. The experience of the detached head is not unusual and when I am more fully present with him and make note of this, it is a useful tool in bringing him back to his present experience.*

*My kinesthetic was really in play today, especially in noting disowned emotions (anger and fear) as well as the knot in my stomach. Wondering aloud about these feelings and body sensations with M. put them squarely back in the center of the room, and allowed her to own them as her own. M. has become more and more able to catch herself when she is avoiding her experience of herself, which is making it easier for me to sit back and allow her process to unfold.*

*S. was trying so hard to avoid her anxiety that much energy was being thrown into the room today. As soon as I noticed my own shortness of breath, I asked S. to stop, slow down and breathe. This really helped the energy to shift, and for S. to come more fully into herself. I stayed aware of any time that I felt my breathing get shallow, as a good somatic indicator of S.'s attempt to move out of the present moment.*

**What did I see (experience) in the client? Somatically? Emotionally? Cognitively? Spiritually?**

*J. was very cut off from himself today, which of course I mirrored quite well! I was very aware of him talking from his head and from the past, but having no sense of being in his body or his emotions. This, of course, affected his ability to make sense of his stories, which then kept him spinning in his two-dimensional storytelling rather than being able to move into his here-and-now experience, which would have provided an opportunity to fully engage in his experience and make meaning from it. S. tends to be stuck in his cognitive domain, so this is no surprise, and will be a major focus of our work.*

*Today's session with M. was quite powerful, and except for moments when she tried very hard to avoid her feelings and body sensations, M. was able to be very present with both her feelings and her physical sensations. In allowing herself to be so present as she shared her experience with her father, M. was able to make sense of her in-the-moment experience in session, and come to some realizations of how her father doesn't really see and hear her, as well as of her unrealistic expectations that things are going to change. It was a potent session to witness her truly acknowledging her experiences of herself as real and valid! M. is often stuck in her soma, without being able to connect body sensations to feelings and thoughts. Today she was more able to make those connections without my help.*

*S. over-utilizes her emotional domain more often than not. Today, even her emotions were overwhelmed by her anxiety such that she was having an equal amount of body responses and flights to her head. She would react to her physical discomfort by spinning stories about how out of control her life was. These were distortions of what was really going on, especially in her resistance to seeing how she set herself up for failure by over-scheduling her day. The more I was able to help her center and focus, the better able she was to be present, and begin to reflect on who she was in the moment, and how she was self-sabotaging her life.*

# Final Thoughts

I am a firm believer that the most important aspect of working with clients is to avoid categorizing them in any way that imprisons them in language that does not respect the natural unfolding of our authenticity as human beings. I truly believe that within the confines of our fate and destiny (see my earlier discussion in Chapter 1), our primary drive is towards wholeness and homeostasis. As such, this drive for authenticity is a powerful motivator in allowing our full potentiality to emerge despite and in support of any biological, environmental, and social forces that we have no control over. This is captured in the concept of "self-as-process", and the understanding that who we are in this moment is not who we were in the last moment or who we can be in the next. While having a framework for understanding the etiology of the suffering our clients and we struggle with at any point in time is important, avoiding any compartmentalization and categorization, which freezes a human being in time works counter to an embracing humanistic orientation.

It is my hope that by introducing you to the theory and practice of Contextual Existentialism might give you a new framework from which to understand and work with your fellow travelers in life. It has been almost seven years since I first started working on this book. What I thought would be a one to two year process has evolved into something so much more. This additional time, while more a product of a busy life than anything else, still produced some unintended results. I was able to get much more feedback from a diversity of graduate students and colleagues than I had planned, as well as the additional time allowed for longer and deeper incubation periods. The sum of this all was the ability to allow the structure and flow of this book to shift and change as my ideas and experiences deepened. Of course, it also allowed me to continually edit as more ideas surfaced (or more typos showed up).

Initially I had thought of adding additional chapters on ways in which I believe a Contextual Existential frame might contribute to our understanding of both teaching and organizational work, and perhaps to what I see as overlapping concepts within fields such as Ecopsychology. While I still have interest in these areas, and no doubt will write about them in some context, I concluded that keeping this book's focus on clinical work made much more sense. However, I will continue to consider the ways in which the Contextual Existential frame might allow for understanding of issues and concerns beyond the clinical box. I know that for me, it will be the beginning of an opportunity to move my work forward in some new and interesting ways. I have no doubt that as I continue to work with these ideas myself that a deeper and fuller sense of the human experience and thus both clinical and non-clinical applications will emerge. Future editions of this book will allow me to expand in those areas where this knowledge and experience is illuminated.

In the meantime, I encourage you to think "beyond the box" as well, and to work with the concepts and practices outlined in this book in your clinical work and beyond. To that end my dear reader, I wish you well, stay present, and breathe!!

# References

Adler, A. (1927/1992). *Understanding human nature.* England: One World Publications.

American Psychological Association (2000). *Diagnostic and statistical manual of mental disorders* (4$^{th}$ ed., text revision). Washington, DC: Author.

Barrett, W. (1958). *Irrational man.* New York: Anchor Books.

Becker, E. (1973, 1997). *Denial of death.* New York: Free Press.

Benoit, H. (1990). *Zen and the psychology of transformation.* Rochester, VT: Inner Traditions.

Bergson, H. (2002). *The creative mind: An introduction to metaphysics.* New York: Citadel.

Buber, M. (1970, 1996). *I and thou.* New York: Touchstone.

Bugental, J. (1987). *The art of the psychotherapist.* New York: W. W. Norton.

Epstein, M. (1995). *Thoughts without a thinker.* New York: Basic Books.

Frager, R., & Fadiman, J. (2005). *Personality and personal growth (6$^{th}$ ed.).* Upper Saddle River, NJ: Pearson/Prentice Hall.

Frankl, V. (1959/1984). *Man's search for meaning.* New York: Touchstone.

Freud, S. & Strachey, J. (1962). *The ego and the id (The standard edition of the complete psychological works of Sigmund Freud).* New York: W. W. Norton.

Fromm, E. (1949/1964). *Escape from freedom.* New York: Henry Holt and Company.

Fromm, E. (1956/2000). *The art of loving.* New York: Perennial.

Gendlin, E. (1981). *Focusing.* New York & Toronto: Bantam Books.

Goleman, D. (1988). *The meditative mind: The varieties of meditative experience.* New York: The Putnam Group.

Hays, P. (2001). *Addressing cultural complexities in practice: A framework for clinicians and counselors.* Washington, DC: American Psychological Association.

Heidegger, M. (1962). *Being and time.* San Francisco: Harper.

Hirai, T. (1989). *Zen meditation and psychotherapy.* New York: Japan Publications.

Horney, K. (1945/1972). *Our inner conflicts.* New York: W. W. Norton.

Husserl, E. (1931). *Ideas.* (W.R. Boyce Gibson, Trans.). London: George Allen & Unwin.

Kabat-Zinn, J. (1994). *Wherever you go there you are.* New York: Hyperion.

Kierkegaard, S. (1986). *Fear and trembling.* London & New York: Penguin.

Klein, M. (1957). *Envy and gratitude.* New York: Delacorte Press.

Kockelmans, J. J. (Ed.). (1967). *Phenomenology.* Garden City, NY: Doubleday.

Lauer, Q. (1967). On evidence. In J. J. Kockelmans (Ed.), *Phenomenology.* Garden City, NY: Doubleday.

Levinas, E. (1967). Intuition of essences. In J. J. Kockelmans (Ed.), *Phenomenology.* Garden City, NY: Doubleday.

May, R. (1983). *The discovery of being.* New York: W. W. Norton.

Merriam-Webster Online. (n.d.). Merriam-Webster online dictionary. Retrieved August 1, 2007, from http://www.m-w.com.

Moustakas, C. (1990). *Heuristic research.* Thousand Oaks, CA: Sage.

Moustakas, C. (1996). *Loneliness.* Northvale, NJ & London: Jason Aronsen.

Moustakas, C. (1997). *Relationship play therapy.* Northvale, NJ & London: Jason Aronsen.

Nietzsche, F. (1978). *Thus spake zarathustra.* London & New York: Penguin.

Polanyi, M. (1969). *Knowing and being.* Chicago: University of Chicago Press.

Rogers, C. (1989). *The art of counseling.* New York: Gardner Press.

Sartre, J. P. (1945/1976). *The wall and other short stories.* New York: New Directions.

Sartre, J. P. (1947/1976). *No exit and three other plays.* New York: Vintage Books.

Sartre, J. P. (1993). *Being and nothingness.* New York: Washington Square Press.

Satir, V. (1967). *Conjoint family therapy.* Palo Alto, CA: Science & Behavior Books.

Satir, V. (1988). *The new peoplemaking.* Palo Alto, CA: Science & Behavior Books.

Suzuki, D. T. (1964). *An introduction to Zen Buddhism.* New York: Grove Press.

van Deurzen-Smith, E. (1988). *Existential counseling in practice.* London: Sage.

Vontross, C. (1979). Cross-cultural counseling: An existential approach. *Personnel and Guidance Journal, 58,* 117-122.

Vontross, C. (1999). *Cross-cultural counseling: A casebook.* Alexandria, VA: ACA.

Whitaker, C. M., & Keith, D. V. (1981). Symbolic-experiential family therapy. In A. S. Gurman & D. P. Kniskern (Eds.), *Handbook of family therapy.* New York: Bruner/Mazel.

Winnicott, D. W. (1971). *Playing and reality.* New York: Basic Books.

Yalom, I. (1980). *Existential psychotherapy.* New York: Basic Books.

# Index

Addictions, 18-19
Anxiety, 1-7, 19, 21-27, 63, 68. *See
also* Healthy anxiety *and*
Neurotic anxiety.
  clinical examples, 54, 55-56, 64,
70, 72-74, 77, 80, 81, 86, 91-
96
Assessment, 7, 10, 13-14, 17, 18,
23, 29, 30, 34, 38, 41, 47-58,
59, 61, 62, 63, 65, 67, 69, 70,
79, 81, 86, 87, 99
Authenticity, 5, 8, 16, 17, 21, 23,
25, 27, 36, 37, 41, 45, 46, 48,
49, 50, 63, 64, 65, 67,68, 75,
79, 81, 84, 95, 97, 106
  clinical examples, 70, 72-73, 77,
95

Background. *See* Foreground and
background.
Balance, 3, 4, 7, 8, 10, 14, 17, 24,
25, 26, 48, 49, 50, 63, 68, 70,
72, 75. 78, 79. *See also*
Homeostasis
  clinical examples, 55, 58, 75
Both/and thinking. *See* Paradoxical
thinking
Buddhist concepts. *See* Zen
Buddhism, Non-attachment

Clinician as a tool, 67, 75-76, 79,
84, 97. *See also* Foreground
and background.

clinical examples, 56-58, 76, 98
Communication issues in couples,
87
Congruent living. *See* Authenticity.
Contextual Existentialism, 1-18,
23, 25, 29-31, 35-38, 39, 40,
41, 44, 47, 48. 49, 51, 53, 54,
58, 61, 62, 63, 65, 67, 68, 69,
70, 75, 76, 77, 78,. 79, 83, 85,
100, 106
  definition of, 17-18
Contextual experience, 48, 83, 86,
87, 89
  clinical examples, 34-36, 67, 74,
96
Countertransference, 41, 77
Cultural considerations in
    development of existentialism,
1, 2, 3, 4, 29, 35
Cultural context. *See* Culture.
Culture, 7, 14, 15, 16-17, 18, 22,
23, 25, 26, 29, 30-31, 35, 37,
45, 48, 50, 59,60, 62, 63, 67,
74-75, 78, 83, 96-97,
  ADDRESSING model, 30, 52,
53, 67, 84
  clinical examples, 34, 35, 38, 42,
43, 53-54, 55, 67-68, 69-70,
84, 96-97
  definition of, 30

Diagnosis, 13-14, 18, 59-65
  clinical example, 63-64

Index

Domains of being-ness, 10, 40, 45,
    86
  body/soma, 10, 40, 45, 50,
  clinical examples, 55, 57, 71, 73,
    87, 97, 104
  emotions, 10, 40, 45
  mind, 10, 40, 45
  spirit, 10, 40, 45
Domains of the world
  clinical examples, 55-58, 70, 86
  Eigenwelt, 9, 35, 48, 49, 62
  Mitwelt, 9, 35, 48, 49, 62
  Umwelt, 9, 35, 48, 49, 62
  Überwelt, 9, 35, 48, 49, 62
Dualistic thinking, 16, 19, 78
  clinical examples, 74, 78, 87, 95
Dysfunctional behaviors, 19-20, 22

Early childhood development, 6-8,
    18
Either/or thinking. See Dualistic
    thinking
Existential anxiety, 44
Existential paradoxes, 5, 10, 13, 17,
    19, 23-27, 41, 44, 48-49, 61,
    70, 86
  choice and responsibility, 24, 36
  clinical examples, 4-5, 33-36, 43-
    45, 54, 55, 70-72, 86, 87-89,
    89-91
  death and striving for life, 25-26,
    87-89
  isolation and connection, 7, 24-
    25, 31, 33-36, 71-72, 89-91
  meaning and meaninglessness, 8,
    9, 26-27
Existential thinking
  development of, 2-4

Family systems theories, 83
Foreground and background, 10,
    13, 31, 51-53, 70, 86, 102
  clinical examples, 53-58, 70-71,
    86-87
Frankl, Victor, 3, 8, 21, 47

Freud, 3, 6

Hays, Pamela. See Culture—
    Addressing model.
Healthy anxiety, 7, 8, 10, 17, 18,
    22, 26, 49, 62, 68, 75
Healthy guilt, 49
Heidegger, Martin, 2
Here-and-now experience, 4-6, 13-
    14, 18, 22, 27, 33, 41, 44, 49,
    51, 52, 61, 67, 68, 69, 70, 75,
    79, 80, 83, 84, 97, 99, 101, 102
  clinical examples, 4, 20-21, 34,
    43, 54, 55, 56, 57, 71, 73, 75-
    77, 78-79, 80, 91, 93, 97, 102-
    104
Homeostasis, 3, 4, 9-12, 17, 40, 48,
    49, 50, 67, 68, 81, 84, 106
  clinical examples, 35, 73
  differences with balance, 10
Horney, Karen, 7, 25, 31-32, 35,
    38. See also Relational
    development

Intuition, 15, 18, 39, 40, 44, 50
Intuitive sense
  auditory, 15, 39, 45, 46
  clinical examples, 42-44, 57, 77,
    98, 104-105
  gustatory, 15
  kinesthetic, 15, 39, 44, 45-46, 57,
    76, 94, 98
  olfactory, 15
  visual, 15, 39, 45, 46, 94
Intuitives, 15, 39-44, 76-77, 79, 80,
    81, 97.

James, William, 3

Kierkegaard, Soren, 2, 38, 67, 95
  choice and responsibility, 36
  levels of existence, 8, 36-37

Levels of existence, 8, 36-37, 40
  aesthetic, 8, 36, 73-74

ethical, 8, 36, 38, 74, 94-95
religious, 8, 36
religio-spiritual, 36, 37, 38, 95
clinical examples, 38, 55, 58, 71,
73-74, 87, 94-96
Living authentically. *See*
Authenticity.

Metaphor, 21, 25, 26, 46, 50-51, 94
clinical examples, 57, 92
Mindfulness, 9, 14-15, 18, 21, 41,
clinical example, 64
Moustakas, Clark, 3, 15, 39
Multiplicity, 19, 22-23

Naming, 40, 41, 44, 46, 79, 81, 84,
98
clinical example, 80-81, 99-100
Native American concepts and
practices, 9, 14, 15
Neurotic anxiety, 7, 8, 10, 16, 17,
18, 22, 24, 26, 35, 44-45, 49,
62, 64, 68, 70, 71, 75, 81, 97
Neurotic guilt, 49-50
Nietzsche, Frederich, 2, 8, 39
Non-attachment, Buddhist concept
of, 20, 95
clinical example, 20-21

Paradoxes of living. *See* Existential
paradoxes.
Paradoxical thinking, 6, 15-16, 18,
19, 23, 47, 58, 59, 63, 65, 74,
78, 98.
Paradoxical experience, 21-23
clinical example, 21
Potentiality, 2, 5, 16, 17, 26, 32, 36,
39, 45, 48, 49, 50, 62, 65, 68,
73, 74, 81, 106
clinical examples, 20, 21, 35, 44,
70
Psychoanalytic theory, 3, 6-7

Relational development, 6-7, 18,
31-36

clinical examples, 33-36, 38, 71
Relational styles, 7, 25, 31-33, 35,
86
clinical examples, 33-34, 55, 72,
87-89, 89-91
compulsive compliance, 7, 32, 72
compulsive detachment, 7, 32,
87-89
compulsive aggression, 7, 32, 55,
89-91

Sartre, Jean-Paul, 2, 29
Satir, Virginia, 83, 87
Self
concept of, 16, 20
false sense of, 97
Self as instrument. *See* Clinician as
tool.
Self as process, 74, 106
Self as static, 16, 20, 50, 75
Self-awareness, capacity for, 4, 17,
36, 48, 54, 61, 64, 73
Self-in-relation, 31, 37, 39, 45, 46,
48, 95
Self-transcendence, 2, 18, 27, 37,
44, 45, 48, 49, 73, 74, 75, 95,
96.
clinical examples, 38, 64, 87
Session notes, 101-102
Spirituality, 3, 4, 8-9, 16, 24, 25,
26, 30, 35, 37, 45

Tacit knowing. *See* Intuition.
Therapeutic relationship, 13, 15,
18, 52, 68, 76, 78, 79, 99, 10
clinical examples, 69-70, 72, 78,
85-86
Transference, 13, 15, 40, 41. 84.
*See also* Transferential energy.
Transferential energy, 40, 41, 77-
79, 81, 86, 97, 100, 102
clinical examples, 78-79, 97, 99

Values development, 8, 18, 36-38, 86. *See also* Levels of existence.

Vontross, Clement, 29

Ways of relating to the world. *See* Domains of being-ness.

Whitaker, Carl, 83

Yalom, Irvin, 3, 13, 23, 25, 27, 63, 96

Zen Buddhism, 9, 14, 15, 16, 19, 20-21, 27, 95, 97

# About the Author

Ned Farley is a core faculty member and the chair of the Masters in Mental Health Counseling Program, as well as the chair of the Masters in Integrative Studies in Psychology program in the School of Applied Psychology, Counseling, and Family Therapy at Antioch University Seattle. He has been on the faculty at Antioch Seattle since 1992. Dr. Farley has worked in community mental health, and has been in private practice since 1984. He received his undergraduate training in Theatre and Psychology at the University of Washington, his Masters degree in Clinical Psychology and Mental Health Administration from Vermont College of Norwich University, and his Doctorate in Existential Psychology from The Union Institute & University. He has published articles in journals, chapters in edited books, and is currently the editor of the Journal of LGBT Issues in Counseling, published by Taylor and Francis.